India Served and Observed

Mildred Archer, India, 1976

William Archer, India, 1976

India Served
and Observed

by

William and Mildred Archer

Introduction by Giles Eyre

BACSA

PUTNEY, LONDON
1994

Published by the British Association
for Cemeteries in South Asia (BACSA)

Secretary: Theon Wilkinson MBE
76½ Chartfield Avenue
London SW15 6HQ

ISBN 0 907799 53 1

Cover: A detail from Thomas Daniell's painting of Cleveland House, Bhagalpur
(see full picture on page 83).
Acknowledgements to British Library, OIOC.

Typeset by: Professional Presentation, 3 Prairie Road, Addlestone, Surrey

Printed by: The Chameleon Press Ltd., 5-25 Burr Road, Wandsworth SW18 4SG

Contents

❦ ❦ ❦ ❦ ❦

Note on BACSA. The British Association for Cemeteries in South Asia was formed in 1976 to preserve, convert and record old European cemeteries. All proceeds from the sale of this book go towards this charity (regd. no. 273422).

Illustrations

'Tail-pieces' to various chapters are examples of Bihar toys

❦ ❦ ❦ ❦ ❦

* acknowledgements to the British Library, Oriental & India Office Collections

Photographs from WGA's private collection and mostly taken by him

Foreword and Acknowledgements

"India Served and Observed" is the twenty-fourth in a series of books about Europeans in South Asia, written by BACSA members, published by BACSA for BACSA members but with a wider public in mind, particularly those with a love of Indian Art and an interest in the impact of Europe on Asia - and *vice versa* - politically, socially and artistically,in the final years of the 'Raj'.

This joint autobiography by Dr Mildred Archer ('Tim' to her friends) and her husband, the late Dr William Archer ('Bill') was compiled over a period of years following their return from India in 1948, and is based on a collection of papers and letters. For a number of years before his death in 1979, Bill had been working intermittently on a book of memoirs and the completed sections are included here. He has recorded details of his time as an ICS officer, mainly in Bihar, from 1931 to Independence while Tim has added descriptions of their life together from her own unconventional viewpoint. Later, in England, their development as authorities in their own right on the Indian Art field, with international reputations, needs no elaboration here apart from taking the opportunity to produce a comprehensive bibliography for each of them which lists not only their books but also all their more important other writings.

The writer of the introduction, Giles Eyre, comes from a family with East India Company connections stretching back to its earliest days. He served in the 19th Lancers in India and Malaya from 1942 to 1947, and after the War was ADC to the last two British Governors of the Punjab. In 1968 the gallery of Hartnoll & Eyre opened in Duke Street, St James, and Giles found himself specialising increasingly in oils and watercolours of Anglo-Indian interest. It was in this period that he first met the Archers. After Bill's death, Giles went into partnership with Charles Greig, first in Bond Street and then at Eton. Both partners have travelled extensively in India, and in 1991, jointly with Dr Chakrabarti, produced for the Victoria Memorial, Calcutta, its first catalogue of paintings since 1925; a remarkable collection of great topographical and historical interest. By this time Tim had emerged as an authority on Anglo-Indian Art second to none, and Giles' friendship with them both over this extended period made him an obvious choice to write this Introduction and Postscript, for which BACSA is most grateful.

BACSA wishes to place on record its thanks to the Archer family for entrusting the publication of this important book to us. Thanks are also due to the British Library, Oriental and India Office Collections (formerly the "India Office Library & Records") for their ready assistance.

Introduction

by Giles Eyre

Bill Archer was born in 1907, and went up to Cambridge in 1926. He joined the ICS in 1931 and was posted to his first choice of province, Bihar. Mildred Bell was born in 1911 and educated at St. Hilda's, Oxford. Both were the children of teachers and had gone to day-schools in London. She was introduced to Archer by her brother, Frank, who was a friend of his at Cambridge. They became engaged, but could not get married for several years. Mildred (whom I shall hereafter call Tim, her nickname by which she is better known), was working for her degree, and the ICS did not encourage a junior officer to get married in his first years of service.

The period after 1919 was one of the low points in recent British history. In the face of mounting economic troubles, there was perhaps too much caution and too little inspiration in high places. 1923 had been a milestone in the history of the Labour Party, when Ramsay MacDonald formed a Socialist Government. In a period of depression it did not last, but Labour came in again after the General Strike. It was two years later that Bill Archer got a First in the History Tripos at Cambridge. His mother had just died, and his father followed her shortly afterwards. Bill's last years at Cambridge were clouded by their deaths. 'I threw myself into some of the hardest work I have ever done.' 1930 was the year that Tim won her scholarship to St. Hilda's. They first met in London where Bill was studying Hindi, and Hindu history and law, at the School of Oriental Studies (now the School of Oriental and African Studies - SOAS).

Tim was meanwhile enjoying her life at Oxford, which was alive with left-wing personalities. At that time, the Russia-orientated enthusiasms of Beatrice and Sidney Webb were fashionable. Freedom for India was much discussed, particularly when Gandhi visited the city to receive his honorary degree. During the same period Bill was strongly influenced by Bernard Shaw and Bertrand Russell. His emotional response was also aroused by an early study of Indian art and literature. It is interesting that when he was asked by the examiners at his viva voce why he wanted to go to India, he replied 'Because I want to be stimulated by a new culture.'

By 1931, anyone joining the ICS was in a new and difficult position. Many of the old certainties had disappeared and the political environment was more de-stabilised. To some, the possibility (not the probability) of an early termination of career had to be entertained. In the event, Bill was to be involved in a novel process of handing over power to India. But he could hardly have realised then that such would one day be the spring-board for a very different and fruitful future.

Given some linguistic ability - after an intensive course in spoken and written Hindi - a young ICS officer had to get down to understanding the ways of the Indians whom he was to govern. If he enjoyed Indian food, and accepted Indian hospitality with pleasure - as unquestionably Bill did - the rapport established was particularly valuable. In the next period of training, it was likely that he would be left to administer a district. In Bihar and in Bill's case, he was freer than most to follow his own inclinations. Much of the time he was in the wilder parts, where it was sometimes wiser to follow Indian precedent, while keeping within the framework of British law. In such a way, Bill chose to be guided by his own moral sense - even if colonial tradition sanctioned otherwise. Philip Mason (Woodruff) explains it perfectly: 'There must be no personal advantage to himself of a pecuniary kind, and nothing must be put in writing that would bring a blush to the cheek of a High Court Judge'.

The province of Bihar is divided by the Ganges. The northern districts had been celebrated for their indigo plantations - long since unprofitable. South Bihar was a rice-growing area, dotted with hills and mango groves. Patna, the capital, was on the south bank of the great river. To the south-east were the Rajmahal hills and the Santal Parganas. Even farther south was Ranchi, the chief city of Chota Nagpur.

Bill reported to headquarters in Patna, and at first cordially disliked this colonial city. Together with an Indian servant, carefully chosen for him by the wife of the Commissioner, he departed for Arrah, his first posting, which ironically was celebrated for a brave incident in the uprising of 1857. The Collector, to whom he was apprenticed, was 'a bluff and somewhat eccentric man', about to retire and working on a life of Warren Hastings. At the end of 1932, Bill became Assistant Magistrate and Collector (on training) at Ranchi. Situated on a high plateau, the town contained the residences of senior officials, law courts and schools. The surrounding scenery was more attractive with its undulations, abrupt hills and forest tracks. Rural India was to prove the main stimulus to Bill, and it was in the environs of Ranchi that his expatriate happiness began. He discovered the Santals, a tribal people who had begun to move into the hills and forests at the end of the 18th century. It was their culture and customs which first attracted Bill's sympathy. Many other tribals inhabited Chota Nagpur, and in the Ranchi district they generally were in a majority. Of the smaller tribes, the Oraons, who spoke a Dravidian language, and were of great antiquity, increasingly appealed to Bill. His first book (1940) was a sensitive translation of Oraon songs. It included a scholarly introduction, the first of many studies of tribal culture.

Bill's future postings were to form something of a pattern, and perhaps chosen to match his unusual abilities. However, it is also probable that some character comment had accompanied Bill to Bihar. He was certainly known to be engaged before he left England. The political predilections of Mildred Bell at Oxford, if known, may have raised an eyebrow in Patna. Bill was at Ranchi until the spring of 1933, when he was appointed Joint Magistrate and Deputy Collector at Madhubani in northern Bihar. He was now in charge of a subdivision and could exercise authority in comparative freedom. His closest colleague was a young Bengali in the Police. Mullick was 'clever, sophisticated, resourceful and about my age.' It is clear that they clicked at once.

Some forty years later, Bill was to write a letter to a friend about the background to his development as a collector and scholar in India:

> 'I was posted to Bihar from 1930 to 1946 where I lived the life of a district officer, happiest when out in the Indian countryside, trying or settling criminal and civil disputes, actively concerned with village welfare and in sharp contrast to other members of the ICS in Bihar, warmly friendly with Indians and positively pro-Congress in its campaigning for Indian independence. I was the very opposite of aloof'.

He explains that it was this pro-Indian attitude and feeling which resulted in his introduction and acceptance by certain Hindus and Muslims who shared his aesthetic and intellectual tastes. Also in this period he met Gandhi and travelled, on leave, to Santiniketan to meet Tagore. He was introduced to Kalighat painting, and to two Hindu collectors whose influence was to prove important later.

On the sea voyage out, Tim had met several memsahibs of the type she had read about in *A Passage to India*. They talked to her of 'the Club' and the importance of playing Bridge. They teased her about her left-wing views, and probably relished the thought that such would not last long once she settled down in Bihar. The Headmaster of the Zillah school at Ranchi was on board, and a High Court Judge returning to Patna. They landed in Bombay, and Tim's brother, Frank, was to surprise them in Ranchi where he had travelled to meet them from Bengal. It was several years since he had seen his sister, and there were many things to discuss. One was probably the cost of living in India. In the 1930s, when even a small private income gave an independence in England, the salary of a junior in the ICS provided for an enjoyable 'train de vie'. Polo ponies were unlikely to feature in Bill's budget, so they could probably save something for the future.

Back in Gumla, 70 miles west from Ranchi, Bill took over charge from his predecessor and Tim soon found time for her own pursuits. Into her manuscript creeps a controversial sentence about her husband's ICS commitment:

'Moreover he felt it almost a moral duty to test his Labour principles, and work actively towards Indian Independence through humane administration.'

By 'humane' Tim probably meant consideration and compassion for other human beings, but the sentence might not have gone down well in colonial circles for a different reason. Taking Bengal and Bihar together, educated Indian society was famously more critical of British rule than elsewhere in the subcontinent. Whether this was partly a legacy of the uprising in 1857 is arguable, but fifty years later the more articulate Bengalis and Biharis certainly tended to regard the English as socially exclusive and (in the generality), hostile to their political aspirations.

In Bihar, while Hindus and Muslims lived side by side - usually in amity and respecting each others' feelings - quite minor disputes could lead suddenly to violence. This had been true in Mughal times and continues unabated to the present day. Against that background which particularly affected cities and the larger towns, any administration - however humane - was liable to be criticised, whether indigenous or foreign. Except for a later period in Patna, Bill's postings were to places relatively unaffected.

According to Tim, Bill had gone out to India

'with the belief that he would be one of the last generation (ICS) and saw his task as getting to know as many Indian friends as possible.....'

This was admirable, but previous generations had also worked as district officers, doing unseen work in villages, granting remission for failure of crops and loans for the digging of wells. They had settled land disputes and listened patiently to petitions. It was on the rock of this experience that countless ICS officers had also depended for their empathy with real India - and for millions of patient, hard-working and often undernourished cultivators. If Bill was a paragon, so were they.

GM Ray was in the Bihar Service (ICS) at the same time as Bill. Some of his comments are worth quoting:

'The cultural and historical background of the people among whom we were to work and serve was almost entirely neglected..... All this we were supposed to pick up as we went along..... Finally, each of us was presented with a confidential 'Memorandum on the Subject of Social and Official Intercourse between European Officers and Indian Gentlemen'. This pompous publication was dated Ranchi, 1913.'

Obviously Ray thought, with Bill, that little had moved since then.

At Gumla Tim found it little more than a village. In her comparative isolation - and with no domestic chores - she settled down to learning Hindi. It was not long before she discovered two good libraries in Ranchi, and started to read up about the history of the province, and to study archaeology. Later she taught at the High School, helping eventually to edit new and more suitable text books. Her female friends were often Missionaries and the more educated Indian ladies. One visit to the 'Club' was probably enough.

In 1937, Bill was appointed District Magistrate of Purnea, north of the Ganges and the zone nearest Bengal. Purnea town was on the old route to Darjeeling, and the district was little less than 5,000 square miles. With the decline in demand for indigo, the cultivation of jute and sugarcane had long since taken over. Because of the vagaries of the river Kosi, leaving swamps with each change in its course, the district was considered unhealthy. Celebrated for *shikar* - huge tigers, leopards and even rhinoceros - this aspect had no interest for Bill. Tim's succinct comment was 'utter change from Chota Nagpur'. It does sound rather 'fin de la route' but not without Anglo-Indian interest. By then that term had replaced Eurasian as a euphemism. In and around the somewhat 'dégringolé' capital lived several interesting planter families, some of whom, in the years since the indigo boom, had either been in gentle decline or had intermarried with non-Europeans. There were two clubs which this time had to be visited, the older and more genteel was sad, the other was more convivial, and definitely more Indian. Tim was also to experience her first 'steamy' hot weather and in conditions very different from Gumla. Their son, Michael, had been born in the hospital at Ranchi. His parents now lived in a large early 19th century bungalow with pillared verandahs and a 'porte-cochère.' This stood in its colonial splendour, surrounded by a large compound of greenery. Michael was too young perhaps to remember the flying foxes or the distant hooting of an evening train.

In February 1939, the Archers went on home leave to England, taking Michael with them. It was a fraught period with war looming. When it was declared in September, Bill had to return abruptly and alone. Tim's journey later was a saga, but she and Michael reached Madras safely that December. The month before, Bill had been posted to Hazaribagh which was to be the headquarters for the 1942 census in Bihar, of which he had been placed in charge. Hazaribagh was to the north of Ranchi, centrally placed for touring the entire province. This posting suited Bill's abilities to perfection. 'Census Superintendent Sahib' gave him authority and opportunities to travel very widely. In Bihar, previous census reports in 1922 and 1932 had been in the scholarly tradition. That Bill had already published ethnographical material was a bonus. Far more was involved in India for a census than mere enumeration. Unfortunately Tim had not been well after the birth of their daughter Margaret, nor could she happily leave Michael to travel with Bill. Instead she decided to help with the editing of *Man in India* from Hazaribagh. The district was perhaps the most attractive in the province. The town itself was a quiet back-water, with the atmosphere of an old-world *mofussil* station. In comparison to Purnea, Hazaribagh was higher and had the climate of a health resort.

Meanwhile, Bill heard rumours that after the census he might be posted to Patna. This was confirmed towards the end of 1941, as were his fears that he would encounter there 'the kind of British Indian he intensely disliked.' On arrival they were given a newly-built house on the *maidan* at Bankipore, which was between the old and the new cities of Patna. The new capital of Bihar had been laid out somewhat in the manner of New Delhi, to mark the creation of Bihar as a separate province. The old Patna had contained an English factory, from which Job Charnock left in 1680 to found Calcutta. It still existed as a massive building, now housing the government press. The most conspicuous object in Bankipore was a huge conical-shaped granary, locally known as the Golghar, built in 1786 - less than three decades after Plassey - as an insurance against famine. Up on the stone staircase that encircled it, Michael used to climb to sit at the top and watch the slow-moving boats on the Ganges. In the event, the posting to Patna was to be significant in the Archers' lives, and rather different to what Bill expected.

It was in Bihar, during the 'Quit India' riots of 1942, that the most serious threat to subvert government was organised. Up river, in the Benares Division, HT Lane wrote:

> 'I was disgusted at the wanton destruction of property and above all I was fiercely angry at the obvious attempt to cut communications to the Army in the North East, and thus make it easier for the Japanese to invade India. This change of feeling did not make me any less friendly to my Indian colleagues and private Indian friends, but I grew very cynical about Indian politicians, both local, provincial and national.'

Bill must have known that Bihar was a 'dyed in the wool Congress province'. He had also met Gandhi and would have known that this violence was a betrayal of his ideals. *Satyagraha* was the word that Gandhi had coined for *passive* resistance to British (alien) rule in India. JW Orr (ICS) was in Patna when the Congress high command was arrested throughout the country on 9th August:

> 'When the 10th August dawned, letter-post and telephone no longer operated. With dramatic suddenness and meticulously precise planning the Congress Party had overnight disrupted every form of communication.... not merely between Bihar and the rest of India, but between Patna and any other district headquarters, and even within districts and sub-divisions....'

Tim had been more than eight years in India when the violent 'Quit India' movement caught up with them in Patna. Bill was now Deputy Commissioner and District Magistrate. He had to arrest senior Congress politicians, and see them off in trains into gaol. All this must have been hurtful to them both, but it was Bill who had to represent the Raj. Compassion and sympathy came later, when they sent books and special food to Rajendra Prasad and others in their forced confinement.

That December, Bill was posted as Deputy Commissioner to Dumka in the Santal Parganas - by which time internal peace had been restored throughout the subcontinent. For both, it was to prove an entirely happy and creative period. With the children, they went on tour, slept in tents and could research more fully into the culture, customs and life of the Santals. Years later, this led to the publication of Bill's nostalgic and delightful *Hill of Flutes*. After the Patna experience, Dumka must have seemed a sleepy hollow. It was the headquarters of a district, but 40 miles from the nearest railway station. At nearby Hijla, an annual 'mela' was held - a festive and sporting event for the Santals, accurately described by Tim as a wonderfully virile and attractive people.

They were to be there for the next few years till July 1946 - long after Rangoon had been recaptured from the Japanese. In the intervening years, Wavell had been Viceroy - to be sacked by Attlee a few months later. Before the war, Attlee had commented that 'the idea that Indians must always be ruled for their own good by the lonely white man' was a Victorian sentiment. If the lonely white man was Bill, he was about to be sent in the twilight of the Raj to one of the most outlandish places. The Governor of Assam's adviser had asked for Bill to be loaned to the Naga Hills (Nagaland), as Deputy Commissioner at Mokokchang, because of his tribal experience. He was there 'on the stroke of midnight' when Nehru declared India independent. Although no longer a member of the erstwhile ICS, he stayed on until February 1948 - 'in the vain hope of persuading Nehru to give the Nagas some form of *local* independence.' Frustrated in this, Bill was able to spend two more months in India, visiting museums and staying with Gopi and Krishna Dasa, photographing with his Leica camera hosts of miniatures and preparing himself for a possible museum career.

Bill went to India with a lot of baggage, both ideological and political. It was not that he left without it, but that he had added something more valuable. He had become a collector, and had acquired an aesthetic instinct which he intended to turn to account. The 'eye' in a human being is probably something with which he is born, but the 'infallible eye' is an enhancement of that - developed over a lifetime. In Bill's case, he was to develop it in the next 30 years.

This introduction can only touch on Bill's awakening to the extent and quality - both primitive and sophisticated - in the artistic heritage of the subcontinent. He had been attracted by Indian painting very early on - particularly in London following his Cambridge days - but the scope that then existed in India itself for a discriminating collector came as a considerable surprise. His meeting with several important collectors in this field - both Hindu and Muslim

- was another turning point in his career. His character and good 'eye' equally attracted them. It was on such sincere friendships that Bill was to build in future years for much of his success, first as a curator - to the enrichment of museums - and later as a collector in his own right.

Bill's position in the ICS, from District Officer to Deputy Commissioner in the last decade of the Raj, was unusual. On the one hand he acquired the authority of colonial power, while on the other he doubted the wisdom of the régime which he represented. His political ambivalence was not unique in the last phase of recruiting for the ICS. Long before the war, a weakening had occurred at home of Britain's basic interest in India. Debates in the House of Commons were ill-attended, and there was much liberal-minded sympathy for a Congress party which, in the popular mind, was associated with Gandhi. In the ebb-tide of power and economic advantage after the First World War, talk of the replacement of the Raj was not limited to Socialist circles. Nor was it limited to students up at Oxford or Cambridge. But there was another side to the colonial coin, which Michael Howard gives in *The Lessons of History-*

> 'It involved a sense of mission, a concern for the dissemination of a system of values which, although rooted in one's own nation, were believed to be of universal validity and which was therefore one's duty to spread as wide as possible.'

Acknowledgement is due to Roland Hunt and John Harrison, the editors of "The District Officer in India", 1930-1947 (Scolar Press, 1980) for the quotations by ICS officers in this Introduction.

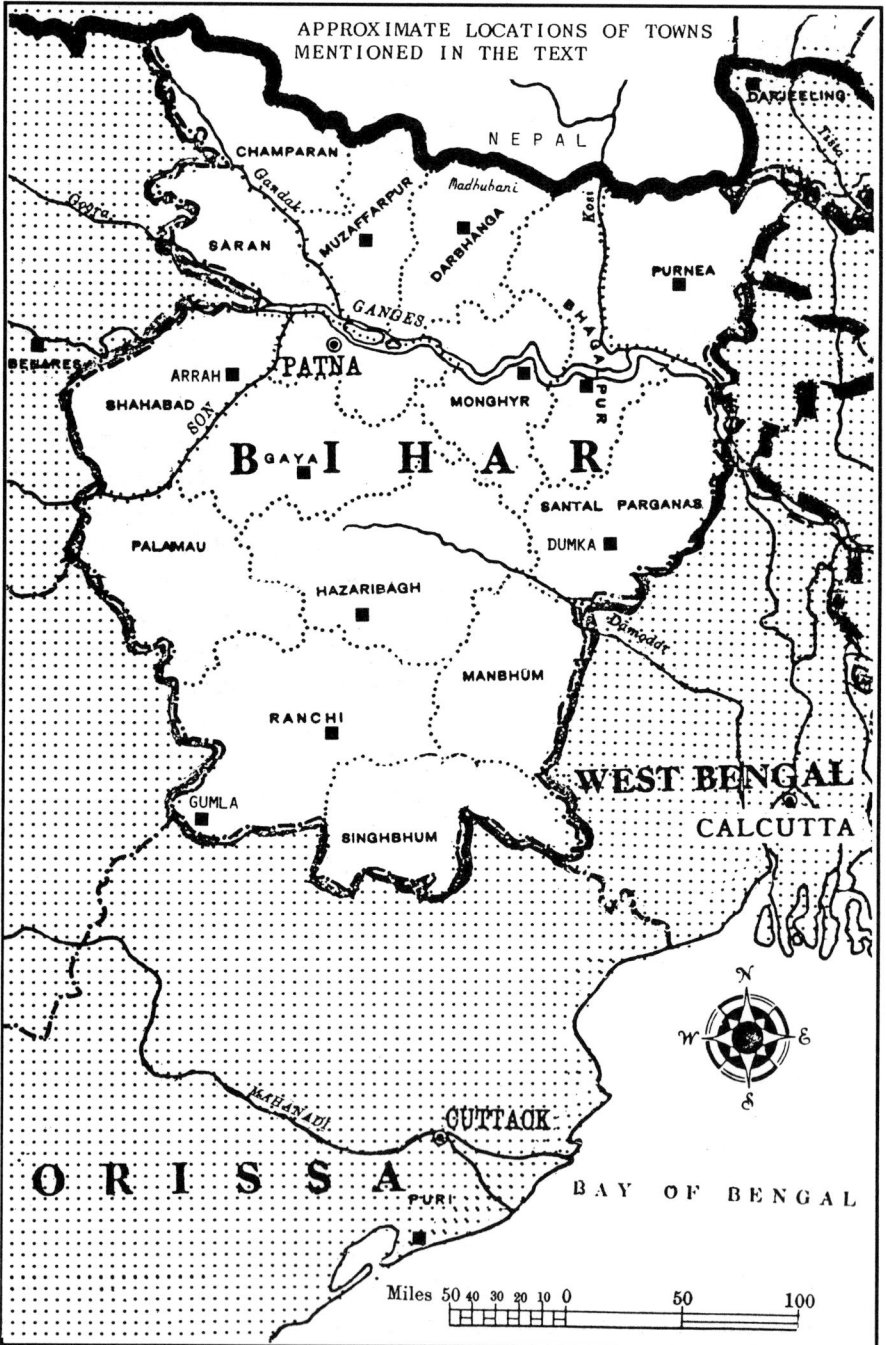

APPROXIMATE LOCATIONS OF TOWNS
MENTIONED IN THE TEXT

NEPAL

DARJEELING

CHAMPARAN

MUZAFFARPUR

Madhubani

DARBHANGA

PURNEA

SARAN

Gandak

Kosi

BHAGALPUR

Ganra

GANGES

BEHARES

ARRAH

PATNA

SHAHABAD

SON

MONGHYR

B GAYA I H A R

SANTAL PARGANAS

PALAMAU

DUMKA

HAZARIBAGH

Damodar

MANBHUM

RANCHI

WEST BENGAL

GUMLA

CALCUTTA

SINGHBHUM

MAHANADI

ORISSA

CUTTACK

PURI

BAY OF BENGAL

Miles 50 40 30 20 10 0   50   100

Inoculation

On 19 October 1934 the P & O liner SS NALDERA docked in Bombay. The experience for which I had been longing throughout the previous four years was about to begin.

In the summer of 1930 William George Archer (Bill, as he was always known), a Cambridge friend of my brother, had passed the exam into the Indian Civil Service and a few months later I won a history scholarship to St Hilda's College, Oxford. During 1930-31 Bill spent his probation year at the School of Oriental Studies in London, learning Hindi as well as Indian History and 'Hindu and Mohammedan Law.' We constantly met and on my leaving school in 1931 we became engaged. Three long years of separation lay ahead of us. At this time Indian Civil Servants were strongly discouraged from marrying during their first years in India and my parents were emphatic that I would be wise first to take my degree before going to India.

In spite of the inevitable strains of separation and the anxious waiting for letters, those years were full of excitement and interest for me. I loved the sheer beauty of Oxford; I thoroughly enjoyed the academic work; a stimulating tutor brought mediaeval history in particular alive for me. I joined the Arts Club and during my first year I spent many afternoons at the Ruskin School of Art learning life-drawing under Albert Rutherston and wood-engraving under Enid Marx. But it was politics, which during 1931-34, largely dominated undergraduate life. It was the depth of the Depression. In 1931 the National Government had been formed, disillusion set in and it was soon despised. Socialism for many of us seemed the only cure for the Depression and the tragic unemployment of the 30s. In my first term I joined the University Labour Club, by far the largest and most active undergraduate society in Oxford at that time. At the first meeting, which I attended, a motion was passed expelling Ramsay MacDonald from his Honorary Presidentship of the Society and I can remember his daughter, Sheila, then an undergraduate at Somerville, hurrying out of the hall in tears. Two young dons, Richard

Crossman and Patrick Gordon Walker held stimulating study groups and encouraged us to join the University Labour Federation. Crossman already showed the brilliance and unpredictable character that remained with him throughout his career. GDH Cole at University College mesmerised us with his stream of publications, his lively lectures and capacity for writing humorous political verse. AD Lindsay, the Master of Balliol, helped to give a philosophical background to our politics through his political theory lectures which included Marxism. It was a period when the young were revolting against the idea that problems could be solved by reason alone. There was a change of emphasis from private to public values and a belief that pre-occupation with the arts and intellectual activities was not enough and there was a resentment of individual privilege. Occasionally we were able to give practical expression to our theories. When the 'Hunger Marchers' stopped at Oxford on their way to London, some of us went to cook for them at Gloucester Green where they were camping. After helping to prepare breakfast for them one morning, I remember walking back to College with Naomi Mitchison, a striking figure in a black cloak and sombrero hat, who animatedly talked about Labour politics and the Haldane family to which she belonged. There was the famous 'King and Country' debate at the Oxford Union when the homosexual Joad recalled Lytton Strachey's response to the question put to Pacifists in the First World War. When asked at his tribunal 'What would you do if a German attempted to rape your sister?' he replied 'I would endeavour to interpose myself between them!' I also remember a great meeting of the Blackshirts when Mosley, accompanied by his wife, Diana, came to Oxford and held a meeting in a hall in Cornmarket Street. When things began to get rough and the police started to throw people out, I prudently decamped!

During my third year I was on the Labour Club Committee with Tony Greenwood, John Cripps, Barbara Betts (later Barbara Castle), and Peter Pain, whose mother was a Wedgwood Benn - names which at that time meant nothing to me. A 'Brave New World' through Socialism seemed to lie ahead. Only the Russian experiment, recommended to us so soberly by Beatrice and Sidney Webb, seemed to offer a hopeful future.

At this time 'freedom' for India was a constant topic of discussion at Oxford. The Simon Commission had sat in 1927, Lord Irwin was Viceroy and establishing a sympathetic relationship with Gandhi who attended the Round Table Conference in 1931. During my first week at Oxford, Gandhi himself visited the city and I stood in the Broad among a great crowd to catch a glimpse of him, a strange wiry figure, wrapped in a home-spun *chaddar*, as he made his way to the Sheldonian where he was to receive an Honorary Degree.

Knowing that I was going to India, I tried to meet as many Indians as possible, so I joined the Majlis, the Indian Society. A number of its members were Indians who had already been recruited to the Indian Civil Service and were spending their two-year probation period in Oxford. I quickly realised that all of them were earnestly looking forward to Independence and the end of British rule, feeling sure that it must come during their life-time. Indeed they justified their entrance into the Civil Service by seeing themselves as the means through which power could be peacefully and efficiently transferred from Britain to India. From them I soon sensed how much they abhorred the superior manner of many of the British in India, especially 'the memsahibs'. I saw a great deal of Humayun Kabir, whom Bill, as an undergraduate at Cambridge, had met at a League of Nations conference in Geneva. Kabir, at Exeter College, was working for his doctorate on Kant during 1931-32. He narrowly missed becoming the first Indian President of the Union by a handful of votes after a recount. I remember him speaking there in May 1932 on the motion 'This house condemns the Indian policy of HM's Government'. Shortly afterwards another Indian, Karaka, became President of the Union. Kabir was eventually to become Minister of Scientific and Cultural Affairs (1958-63) in Independent India and remained one of our closest friends until his early death in 1966.

A number of meetings at the Labour Club were devoted to the subject of India. HN Brailsford, author of *Rebel India* (1931), spoke there as well as Krishna Menon and the indomitable little Ellen Wilkinson, both of whom had been members of the delegation sent to India by the India League. They addressed the Club after the publication of their report *The Condition of India*, in 1932. The Quaker, Reginald Reynolds, on returning from his visit to India, also came to speak and arrived dressed in *khadi* with a Gandhi cap, carrying a lathi to illustrate the 'brutality' of the Indian police, 'those henchmen of the Raj'! Many books on India were in wide circulation at this time, especially Edward Thompson's *The Other Side of the Medal* (1925) and *The Rise and Fulfilment of British Rule* (1934). Looking back after more than 60 years' acquaintance with India, I realise that these speakers and writers greatly over-simplified the political situation and greatly exaggerated the repressive aspects of British rule; but I nevertheless still think that their agitation was necessary and justified. I still believe that my deep love of India and happy

3

relationship with so many different types of Indian resulted from the liberal attitudes that I imbibed at Oxford during those formative years and the friendships that I made there. Although the Oxford Labour Club was a comic mixture of childish fun and naive idealism, it aroused a serious interest in India where a number of these future civil servants and politicians were later to play a prominent role. Although at Christmas parties we might sing a parody of the 'Darkie's Sunday School':

> 'Red Shirts, Black Shirts, everybody come,
> Join the Oxford Labour Club and make yourselves at home,
> Bring your Marx and Engels and sit upon the floor,
> And we'll teach you economics that you've never heard before.

after the weekly meetings when the Committee members would migrate to the Mitre or Kemp Hall for drinks with the speaker of the evening, there was serious argument and discussion which eventually played its part in the legislation and reforms of the post-war years in which a number of these undergraduates were later to be politically involved.

Bill had already come under similar influences at Cambridge between 1926 and 1930. He had been an active member of the Labour Club there and in his third year he had been its Secretary. Indian affairs had not interested him particularly, although through his friendship with Humayun Kabir and Sushil Dey, he had become aware of Indian political aspirations. Until September 1930 he had had no idea that he would actually be going to India: when he sat for the combined Home and Indian Civil Service exam he had had no special preference for either branch, and he would perhaps have preferred to end up in Whitehall, since he felt it would be easier in England to preserve his interests in poetry and art. Like Herbert Read, whom he greatly admired, he half wanted to become a Civil Servant, reserving his leisure time for literary and artistic criticism and for writing poetry. Yet India seemed a not unviable alternative. There was the example of EM Forster's *A Passage to India*. Here was a classic of modern writing based on first-hand experience of India, using Indian material and an Indian setting. Then there was TS Eliot, perhaps the greatest and most sensitive poet of the 30s. He also had his Indian interests. At Harvard he had read Sanskrit and in *The Waste Land* he had introduced Indian imagery and even Indian words as an integral part of his visionary interpretation of modern life. Bill had been mesmerised by that poet's work, and in the poems he himself wrote at Cambridge the influence was evident. If a major novelist and poet had found stimulus in India, it was no wonder that when asked by an examiner at his viva why he wanted to go to India, he replied

4

with youthful pomposity 'Because I want the stimulus of a new culture'. When he took the exam he was in fact torn between the two countries - Britain with its modern art exhibitions, cinema, ballet and poetry and India with its, as yet unknown, culture. Moreover he felt it almost a moral duty to test his Labour principles and work actively towards Indian Independence through humane administration. It was therefore' no great disappointment when he heard that by a strange quirk of fortune, a lump-sum deduction of marks for bad handwriting (two examiners had complained of this) had brought him into the quota destined for India. The probation year which Bill then spent at the School of Oriental Studies aroused his interest in Indian art and literature and directed his activities into new channels which later were to become the consuming passion of both our lives.

When asked if he had a preference for any particular province he opted for Bihar. The Punjab was normally the favourite province with the British, and Bill guessed that that would be the choice of the top entrants or those who had family connections there. On the other hand, if he had said he had no preference then he would probably have been sent to Bengal. (This had happened to my brother, FO Bell, the year before.) With its ugly terrorism and bad climate, Bengal was the most unpopular province in the 1930s. Bihar, from the reading we had done, seemed historically one of the most interesting areas. We were later to discover what a lucky decision this was, for with its varied 'folk art', it was one of the most interesting provinces.

1

Arrival in Patna

To the British members of the Civil Service in Patna, the capital of Bihar, the young man who arrived in November 1931 must have seemed a doubtful acquisition. Chandrapore in Forster's *A Passage to India* was based on Bankipore, a suburb of Patna. The Patna civil station and all that I saw or heard of British attitudes and behaviour in those first few days seemed to confirm Forster's description. I already had two close Indian friends: Sushil Dey, who had preceded me in the Civil Service, and Humayun Kabir. When we had first met in Geneva some years before we had clicked at once and in our general left-wing attitudes and our interest in poetry we had found a common basis for affectionate trust. With two such friends I could not regard Indians as anything but equals. It was monstrous, I thought, that the British should still be ruling India and the only justification I felt for joining the service was that by doing so I could perhaps in a small way give it a more sympathetic face. I determined to mix with Indians freely and equally - to ignore class and caste, and do my best to help the transfer of power to India. My first experience at Patna, however, soon filled me with despair.

The province of Bihar is divided by the Ganges. Entering its territory 100 miles below Benares, the great stream takes its mile-wide course past a series of districts. On its left bank lies North Bihar, formerly studded with indigo plantations, the scene of Mahatma Gandhi's early campaigns, now rich sugar-cane country, yet with its easily flooding rivers, insecure. On the right bank lies South Bihar, a huge level rice-growing area open to the vast sky, the low horizon broken occasionally by little stony hills, palm trees and mango groves, ending to the south in the tumbled uplands of Chota Nagpur and the Santal Parganas.

The old city of Patna itself stretched in a line along the banks of the Ganges, suburb succeeding suburb, till after ten miles to the east the houses suddenly stopped and the road entered park-like country. The eastern suburb, Bankipore, was the headquarters of the district administration. Here the mansions of the local officials, set beside a green *maidan*, had a classical 18th century grace. The University lay to hand. Here the Indian lawyers, doctors and professors had their houses. But it was neither in the city itself nor in Bankipore that I was to stay on arriving.

The province of Bihar had been divided from Bengal in 1912. A separate Government had been appointed, a separate Secretariat had been constituted, and in consequence a new capital had been designed and built. The site stretched for about three miles to the west of the old city and Bankipore. Designed by an English architect, JF Munnings of the Public Works Department, it was insulated from all contact with ordinary Indian life. At one end lay Government House, while down a wide avenue were the High Court, the Council House and the long Secretariat building - its great tower with red-tiled roof dominating the vast expanse. In between were wide, smooth tarmac roads with Government Offices, a Museum, a statue of Lord Hardinge, and lying back behind neat hedges, large brick-built bungalows with trim flower-beds and close cut lawns. In these houses lived various members of the Indian Civil Service, a few Indian, but the majority British. Between this spacious suburb, influenced by British values and housing mainly British people, and the India of the villages and the country towns there seemed not the slightest connection. Driving from Patna City to the New City it was as if you crossed a frontier. You left the province behind and entered an isolated world of unreal quiet and aloofness.

WGA in 1930

I spent my first few days in Patna with feelings of sick dismay. Eager to make contact with Indians at Patna, I had innocently imagined that in my first week I would have met a number and indulged in lively talk. I wanted to like and be liked, to make Indian friends and to feel at ease in Indian society. Yet it was as if the very lay-out of Patna City was intended to thwart all such designs. I stayed with the Chief Secretary, Maurice Hallett, and these four days passed in depressing reactions. It was not surprising that in the closed society which I now entered I met no Indians for, apart from one or two members of my own service and the servants, there were none. I was taken to watch the Governor leave on tour, a red carpet stretching from the pavement to the train. More shattering to my callow hopes, however, had been my first encounter with members of my own Service. Discussing Forster's novel in London, I had been assured that the book was a vicious distortion of the true facts. 'That book', people said, 'is so unfair to the British.' Yet I was taken to the Patna Club, which was still debarred to Indians, and I sensed at once how the general attitude was still one of cold aloofness. You did not meet Indians socially. You governed them. If you were kind to them, they abused it, I was told. Nevertheless you did everything you could for their welfare. But for the rest, your loyalties were to the British. A civil disobedience campaign had been started just before I left England. It was not quite over, but it was being dealt with firmly. It was quite misguided, and was due mainly to a few agitators. No-one in their senses could really think that India was fit for self-government. The Raj had all along been British and British it would and should remain. Besides, who would want to mix socially with Indians? Their interests were not your interests. They had no sense of humour and could be such bores! I had ventured to remark that surely there were some Indians one could get to know. I mentioned how that very morning I had called at the Imperial Bank to open an account and I had had an interesting talk with the young accountant there. He was educated, intelligent and a relative by marriage of Nehru himself. Despite the current political campaign he had shown a friendly courtesy to me and we had had a long talk. If an accountant had been like this surely there must be many others. My hostess looked at me with astonishment. 'I shouldn't see any more of *him*, if I were you'!

Later I realised that behind this aloofness lay a sense of class. The British, whatever their social origins in Britain, immediately joined the upper classes when they entered India. It was the logical corollary to belonging to the same race as the rulers. It was only rajas whose status was comparable, only for them that the social ban should be lifted. Had I known this at the time I might have understood the predominant attitude, but even if I had understood, I could hardly have shared it. I was not prepared to believe that friendship was impossible, intimacy out of the question. To do so would have negated my whole feeling of purpose - for why should I go to India to remain a stranger there? I was left with an unhappy dilemma. If I decided to learn not from experience but from my seniors, I should clearly be more acceptable to the Raj, but viciously false to my own affections and character. Possibly if I had come across a single British official whose approach to India fired me, I might have adopted a different attitude. (That a few civilians with my views existed in other parts of the province I was fortunately later to discover.) As I met the British members of the Indian Civil Service in Patna, I realised that they had little in common with Indians: they had even less in common with me. None were interested in art or poetry. In politics all were Tories. If I was prone to question, they were prone to accept. Even for the current amusements - polo, shooting and bridge - I had no immediate taste. Their reading was not my reading, their values not my values. Nothing then could be gained by accepting their code. You enjoyed the work as a superior amusement. If you had a duty it was to the villagers. They were nameless and remote. I was in for isolation whatever I did, and desperate though the prospect appeared, I decided that I would sooner be friends with Indians at the risk of isolation from British society than cultivate a series of acquaintances like those I had just met.

These then were my first unhappy reflections on arriving in Patna; but I couldn't be unhappy long. On reporting, I learnt that I had been posted as Assistant Magistrate to Arrah. When at last I was in the train travelling the 40 miles to Arrah my spirits rose. Lying on a leather upholstered seat, I was free to ponder my first ten days in India. Around me were piled up the impedimenta which were to accompany me on many later journeys - tin boxes, Marshall trunks (tin-lined with air-tight rubber edges 'to keep the damp and white-ant out'), a hold-all and that indispensable item of equipment - a bedding roll. I had also acquired another appendage - a bearer or general factotum. He was Adwardhan Khan, and one look should have warned me that here was no ordinary servant. Mrs Hallett, wife of the Chief Secretary, had thoughtfully provided me with him. I was relieved and exhilarated at leaving Patna. The weight of senior opinion soon slipped away. Before me lay a little country town where I should soon be learning a fascinating job, soon be living in the India I wanted to know.

9

2

The First Posting - Arrah

Arrah, to which I had been posted in December 1931, was the administrative headquarters of Shahabad, a district to the south-west of Patna. It was a small country town, its only claim to fame being 'the Siege of Arrah House' during the uprising, when in 1857 a small group of English and Eurasians were besieged by a force of mutineers from Dinapore. The men, supported by 50 of Rattray's Sikhs, held out for a week in the hot weather against a large force until they were relieved by Major (later Major-General) Vincent Eyre. The house still stands and the story has been told in many accounts of the events of 1857.

The houses of the District Magistrate and the Judge lay outside the town on a park-like *maidan*. Normally, newly arrived ICS officers were sent to live for the first few months with the District Magistrate so that they could learn at first hand the day-to-day administration of the district and swat for their impending Departmental examinations. However, I was allotted a tiny bungalow to myself. This proved the greatest possible advantage, since although from time to time I felt lonely and isolated, it allowed me to discover India for myself and did not force me on my arrival to identify myself with the small British community stationed there. I became very fond of my Collector*, Mr Peck, who was a bluff and somewhat eccentric man, spending his leisure time not only on the conventional relaxations of the Club and *shikar* which he greatly enjoyed, but working on the life of Warren Hastings, a character whom he greatly admired. (Sadly, Peck died before he could finish and publish his material.) He gave me a strict grounding in administrative work, criticising me at first for making over-heavy weather of the judicial side. But I was left free to make friendships with the local Indian officials and people.

One of these was Sadashiva Prasad, a Deputy Magistrate. He was a deeply religious Hindu of the Kayasth or 'writer' caste, from whom I was able

* 'Collector' - the chief administrator of an Indian district, whose special duty was to collect revenue.

to learn a great deal about orthodox Indian life. Sadashiva remained a firm friend throughout my time in India. Soon after Independence he came to England on a visit and stayed with us at Oxford in 1948. I can still remember hearing him chant his prayers during his early morning bath. His premature death in Patna soon after Independence was a sad blow to us. I also came to know a local pleader, Mr Jain, who taught me a great deal about Indian religion. One day he took me to the local temple. On the way he asked me if I had heard of Hughes of the United Provinces cadre. I said that I'd heard his name. Nirmal told me how he had once met him. They had both lain on the grass in Hughes' garden and they had talked about India. It was obvious how much Nirmal had liked him. I had heard much criticism of Hughes from the British, but he was obviously someone who had found the right Indian niche. What does it matter if a planter's thin imagination calls you 'Bolshi' when your name is circulating over India as an officer whom Indians mention to each other with approving delight? Through visiting the houses of the local people, my activities in Arrah soon made me somewhat suspect with the British officials, especially as it transpired that in the evenings I sometimes changed into Indian dress, wearing a *kurta* (a loose shirt) and pyjamas (loose cotton trousers). I never went out in this dress but word soon spread. I also became interested in Indian music and I invited some of the local people to come and teach me basic *ragas* and *raginis*. Indian dress combined with sounds of music coming from my bungalow led to extraordinary rumours and my first confidential report noted that 'Some of his activities are undesirable'! In fact this early introduction to Indian music stood me in good stead when after Independence I became Keeper of the Victoria and Albert Museum's Indian Department in London and I was involved in the complexity of *raga* and *ragini* subjects depicted in Indian miniature paintings.

During my first Christmas in 1931, I was taken by Peck on a tiger-shooting expedition in Sasaram. I loathed the idea of killing tigers and I was a hopeless shot. When a sambur deer came and stood right in front of my hide, I found my safety catch was still on! But the expedition was important from two points of view. It introduced me to the delights of the Indian countryside in the cold weather and to a great Mughal monument, the nearby Fort of Rohtasgarh, perched on a rocky promontory overlooking the Son River. I climbed up to it and wandered round its magical deserted courts. It also introduced me to Birnath, the Tiger God, about whom I was later to write my book *The Vertical Man* (1947).

11

The Tiger God, Birnath, Arrah district, 1931

3

The Tiger God

The Indian jungle has a strange power of its own. You feel it is occupied even if no-one is there. I first had this uncanny experience when I was taken on the tiger shoot that Christmas. A sandy track led into the jungle which rose in great slopes above us. There was a dry, ominous stillness. Apart from a single vulture high up in the sky, there wasn't even a bird. And then suddenly rounding a corner, I saw a shrine. It consisted of a little round platform and two gaunt standing figures made of stone. They were only about three feet high, but they represented two powerful men, each with a kind of collar round his neck and each with a club or baton in his hand.

A day or so later I saw another shrine. This time the figures were made of wood. They were great erect posts, the top carved to resemble a head, the arms engraved on the post, and once again each with the same enigmatic collar. On speaking to the villagers, I learnt that both were shrines to a godling whose name was Bir Kuar or Birnath, who acted as a kind of warden of the jungle. He did not have the supreme majesty or might of Vishnu or Shiva. He did not reign from above the world. He was part of the jungle and he had two important roles: he protected the cattle from tiger and he ensured that the herds would steadily increase. He did not do this for nothing. He did it in return for respect, recognition and admiration, the admission that although you might not see him, he was all the time there in the jungle, watching the tigers and caring for the cattle. The stone and wooden images were put up to honour and appease him and both were clues to his character. The images also honoured his fertility function by showing him in the form of a *lingam* and *yoni*. The *lingam* is the male organ and the *yoni* the female, and all over India in temples to the great god Shiva, the central image in the shrine consists of a single shaft of stone embedded in an oval shape, the *yoni*. In the wooden posts to Birnath, the godling of the cattle, the post itself represented the *lingam*, and the strange mysterious collar the female *yoni* stressing the godling's intimate function in fertilising the cattle. In the stone images on the

13

other hand the stress was on his vast human power as guardian of the herds, and at first sight you would think that his fertility role had been forgotten. Then you would notice the ruff round the neck which all the images wore. They would stimulate the cattle, make them fertile and thus promote the welfare of the whole village. It is these ideas, which still persist in village India today, that we need to carry with us when we consider classical Indian sculpture.

Around the base of the figures were offerings of little terracotta horses. Like the carpenters who supplied the posts, the potters who modelled these did so as a duty. They were not for sale. They were to provide the god with a steed, a form of celestial conveyance, and thus win his favour.

4

Settlement Work, Ranchi District

That winter, Settlement Training took me from Arrah into the Uraon country in Chota Nagpur. It was as you neared Ranchi that you noticed a great change. It wasn't only the landscape, for the country had already altered on the way there. 100 miles to the north the vast open fields scorched by the huge sky gave place to low hills, to tall scoured rocks. The road passed through jungle, ran out into open country, crossed the Grand Trunk Road and again began to rise, climbing higher and higher into the hills of the Chota Nagpur plateau, a part of Bihar. The *sal* forest spread for miles around. In Bihar, trees were lonely items in a landscape of fields - a row of palm trees, a grove of mangoes, a hoary banyan tree with branches like an octopus. But here in Chota Nagpur, the forest ruled. It swept across the slopes and clothed the hillsides with green. Sometimes it thinned and one saw rice fields descending in long terraces and bare uplands scarred with red soil.

As you neared Ranchi, the whole country came to life. It was no longer drably male. On the plains, in the dusty villages, you hardly ever saw a woman. A few low-caste drabs in filthy clothes, a decayed old beggar searching for scraps - these were all you ever noticed. If you entered a village and the women were about, they hurried into veils and scuttled to shelter, shrank into a twittering nervy silence. On the roads it was only men you saw: men with *lathis*, men with ploughs, men with ponies, men with baskets - always only men. But nearing Ranchi, the road was alive with girls and women as well as men and boys. Those I first saw were all Uraons, a tribal people, coming back from market. The girls wore little bodices and thick white saris edged with scarlet. Their skirts came just below the knee. White flowers were stuck in their glossy hair and as they strode along they laughed and joked with the boys. Sometimes a group were singing as they passed. There was a natural gaiety about the scene. The girls and women were taken for granted. They had a boisterous freedom. There was no longer a sense of huddled shame. You were suddenly face to face with youth and health.

Uraon villagers sharpening a spear-head, 1931

All that winter I camped among the Uraons. Their country spread to the west of Ranchi, the capital of Chota Nagpur, while to the east there lay a narrow band 20 miles in length. It was in this furthest corner that I lived. On the road was a village, Ormanji, which became my general base. I would camp there ten days in the month. The rest of the time I was moving around the country, pitching my tent in a grove of mangoes, halting for two nights and then moving on. The fields were being mapped for revenue purposes, their owners' names recorded, and I had to ride across the uplands to check the survey work and settle disputes. When I started, the harvest was beginning and throughout the day Uraons were working in the fields, cutting the rice and stacking it in stooks. Then a little later they began to move it in and I met boys and girls staggering gaily along as they brought the huge bundles, balanced on their heads, back to the village. As it neared Christmas, the fields grew empty and I rode across the sharp stubble, cracking the dry mud. The sun poured down with a dazzling brilliance, but as it turned to the late afternoon, the hills got darker, the forest began to smoke with mist and I would make for camp, cantering through the cold and shrouding gloom.

It was after dark that I knew the countryside was Uraon. In the early part of the night, a chilly gasping hush would grip the land. Outside my tent the mango trees stood sharp and black against the stars and not a sound would break the night. Then, a little later, brisk and insistent, the drums would start. At first it was a single drum, slowly and firmly beating like a thin command. It would go on firmly calling while the girls and boys gathered after supper.

16

Then with a sharp rub-a-dub-dub other drums would join in; the girls would form a line, their arms around each other's shoulders, and with the steps getting quicker and quicker the whole line would start to wheel around.

Uraon drummers, 1931

One night the moon shone creamy and serene and I could see the rice fields stretching to the shaggy far-off hills. The air was filled with a gentle whitish light and as the drums began I decided to go out and watch the dancing. The path went over the fields, across a tiny shallow river. On the other side was a small hillock and beyond it lay the village. As I neared, the voices of the girls came clearly through the air and from the hillock I watched the scene below. There were only seven girls and three boys. The girls were moving in a line while the boys drummed and capered. They weren't dancing the crops up. They weren't dancing the bride to bed. They were just dancing because they liked it. It was the way to pass the night. The joking songs never seemed to get stale. There were only a few drum rhythms, the dances fitted them - they were made for Uraon bodies. The girls felt free and wild while they danced. The drum rhythms took them out of themselves. They forgot the day's work, the strain of carrying heavy pots of water, the monotony of the thudding rice-pounder up-and-down, down-and-up. All the while the boys were flashing around them with circlets in their hair and red beads around their necks; neat and smart, their eyes full of excitement. I felt a strange exhilaration to be out alone in the night under the shivering sky watching this private scene.

17

5

Madhubani, the First Subdivision

At the end of the cold weather of 1933 I was sent across the Ganges to Madhubani, a subdivision of Darbhanga District in North Bihar, known in mediaeval times as Mithila, the country of the Maithils. It was bordered on the north by Nepal, on the east by Saharsa, a subdivision of Bhagalpur District, and on the south by the Sadr or 'home' subdivision of Darbhanga itself. The headquarters of this district was at Laheriasarai, a mile or so out of Darbhanga town.

It was my first taste of freedom, for as Subdivisional Officer I was now in sole charge of the area. I was responsible for law and order, heard complaints, dealt with petitions and tried the more important cases, inspected roads, schools and hospitals. If there was an emergency, it was I who had to deal with it. I was aided by an Assistant Superintendent of Police who commanded the inspectors, sub-inspectors and constables. He saw that all major crime was investigated and he deployed forces if there was danger of a breach of the peace. I also had a member of the Bihar Provincial Service, a Deputy Magistrate, to help me. He did most of the revenue work and tried most of the criminal cases and also looked after the Treasury. I had a *peshkar* or clerk who put up all judicial papers to me, a *nazir*, another clerk, who served out summonses, and an office superintendent who ran the office, sifted correspondence and put up files to me for orders. Every two weeks I had to send the District Officer a 'Fortnightly Confidential Report' which briefed him on the state of the crops, mentioned any political developments, and in general drew his attention to anything of significance that was happening in the subdivision. He, for his part, sent down to me communications from the Bihar Government and, if necessary, asked me for reports. As Subdivisional Officer I was an *ex officio* member of the District Board, an elected body which administered schools, hospitals and roads. The Board met once a month: I would then go into Laheriasarai, stay with the District Officer, discuss what was happening, and then return to my own domain. In this wider world where bridge and polo were played, life was lived in English style, and English books, English news and English people were discussed; at Madhubani, however, my days were spent entirely in Indian company. It was true, official business was done in English and English was what I normally spoke; but if villagers, litigants or visitors did not speak English, I talked in Hindi. My Hindi was as yet hardly good enough for formal occasions or for public speaking - but in villages where a wide vocabulary and correct grammar were less important, it was effective. I could make myself understood and understand what I heard. In Madhubani town there were no other Europeans and there were none in the subdivisions apart from a few planters and a Manager of the Darbhanga Raj, one of the largest *zamindari* estates in Bihar. With these other Europeans I would make contact from time to time but in my first few weeks I settled down, an Indian among Indians.

My first business, as I saw it, was to get to know my chief colleague, the Assistant Superintendent of Police, a young Bengali, Bhola Nath Mullick. He was clever, sophisticated, resourceful, and about my own age. He was brisk, efficient, cool and brave. He had no illusions about his inspectors and sub-inspectors but, like myself with my clerks, he had come to value his subordinates for what they were. Their manoeuvrings might at times amuse him but he had their measure. He spoke and wrote excellent English and could be very funny and amusing company. We met the first day I arrived and clicked at once. Some of my later interests must have struck him as strangely un-ICS but I never forfeited his generous understanding or support.

The local people presented different problems. I caused them consternation when I took my first seat in court and held my first *sawalkhani*. (Sawal means complaint or petition.) Madhubani was a notoriously heavy subdivision and if you admitted every complaint, you would spend your whole time glued to your courtroom, never stirring out. Maithil Brahmins and Maithil Kayasths were exceptionally clever people, adept at law, and litigation was therefore one of their favourite pursuits and pastimes. 'Police' cases could not be avoided for once a person had been charged he had to be tried. But cases brought by private individuals were different. One had discretion. You could admit the complaint, summon the accused and after his appearance, fix a date for trial. Alternatively, you could send the complaint for local enquiry by a local gentleman, an honorary magistrate, or by someone with whom the complainant was satisfied. You would add the hopeful rider 'for amicable settlement if possible'. The advantage was that it brought the quarrelling parties together, provided them with an arbitrator and with luck enabled them

19

to compose their differences out of court. If it succeeded - and in most cases it did - there was one less case for the over-worked magistrate to try. Finally, you could dismiss the complaint out of hand. It was 'too petty' or 'too trivial', you could maintain: it was not a criminal offence you could rule, though this was more difficult, this is unreasonable and so on. The net result was that while the litigant was sent miserably away the file had been lightened.

I was nothing if not a whole-hogger. If I was to act, I must act firmly. It was not for nothing that my first Collector, Mr Peck, had given me a thorough grounding and had dressed me down for making heavy weather of my first small cases. I did not see myself as a magistrate, or a judge. I loathed the laborious business of writing out in my own hand the evidence. I loathed still more the time-wasting business of writing out a well-argued judgement. Yet one had to do it, as otherwise the Court of Appeal would not uphold it and back it would come with remarks damaging to one's prestige and reputation. It was not for this that I had come to India. I had been warned that in Madhubani on some days there would be as many as twenty complaints filed in court. Twenty cases! Not, of course, to be tried by myself, but by my poor subordinate magistrate. If I issued summonses in each of them, what on earth would he do? I remembered Peck's policy of rueful firmness. I would make my position clear from the start. A genuine case of frankly wrongful conduct, of course I would entertain. But I could not and would not encourage criminal litigation.

The first complainant appeared. I heard him, read his petition, thought for a moment and then with the false bravado of a young batsman, making his first appearance for England in a Test Match, and hitting his first ball for six, I summarily dismissed it. There was a gasp as the assembled pleaders and *mukhtiyars* saw what had happened. The other complaints I heard and disposed of in a calm and undramatic manner. Perhaps things would not be as bad as they looked. They had had a shock, a jolt, a glimpse of a tough and resolute character! They would have to wait a little but with luck I might not prove too savage, ruthless or unreasonable. They would give me a chance but they would have to be wary.

They need not have worried. I had acted as I did only from a sense of desperation, a consuming desire to do good, to identify myself with all that was constructive. I had the welfare of the subdivision at heart. I had been a little tactless but I was not anti-lawyer, and as the days went on, I became more philosophical. I came to enjoy a certain amount of court work and the lawyers themselves became my friends. Their leader was a tall commanding figure,

Rai Bahadur Sushil Kumar Roy known as Sushil Babu (Babu was the equivalent of Mr). A Bengali, he had a soft and soothing personality. He was never rattled. He had a natural politeness. His intellect was first class and whenever he argued a case I knew I was in for a brilliant display of persuasive logic. He was greatly admired in the town, for he fully identified himself with its business. He was Chairman of the Municipality and Vice-Chairman of the local bank. Like everyone else, he was a nationalist at heart but he was not a Congress man. He had never been to gaol but with a kind of serene wisdom he had acted as an emollient. I sensed I had a valued ally. Yet in one respect he was untypical. While he was a man of natural goodness, great integrity and the highest morals, he wore his Hinduism lightly. Almost all the other lawyers in my court were Maithils. Many were Brahmins, and as such one called them 'Pandit this' or 'Pandit that'. Their usual surname was Jha. Others were Kayasths. Whether Kayasth or Brahmin, they were all deeply orthodox Hindus. They took ritual baths in the morning, spent at least an hour at their devotions, said prayers to Vishnu and Shiva, and smeared horizontal lines of sandalwood paste on their foreheads. They were meticulous observers of festivals. All were vegetarians. Compared to the lawyers I had worked with in Arrah, they belonged to an older, more venerable world. They carried with them an aura of ancient culture and custom. Mithila itself was ancient ; it was off the main stream, an aloof, an isolated part of the province, and with a cultured dignity and way of life that I found hard to define. Sanskrit was its very stuff; and although Madhubani town had its Watson HE School (Higher English) and many schools in the district taught English, Sanskrit seminaries were still a common institution. Over everything lay a deep conservatism, a pious regard for unchanging rituals, a firmly unmodern approach to life. It followed that all upper caste Maithil girls and women lived in strict *purdah*: even much later, when I was entertained in orthodox Maithil homes, I would sense that feminine eyes might be watching me but of their owners there was not a trace. It was when I realised how deeply religious my lawyers were that I changed my morning routine. In March, April and May, there was no alternative. We had to start court early since after twelve the heat was so intense, no one could work. But in the Rains and the cold weather, a more civilised regime was possible. I gave up arriving at court at ten. I arrived at ten-thirty and never called a case before eleven. This gave everyone more time and it was proof that I was fast becoming a Maithil.

The lawyers who practised before me had engaging differences of manner. There was 'Lal Babu' with his soft purring manner and merry smile,

Ramchandra Jha with his dignified solemnity, Anup Lal Thakur, gruff of voice but eager not to waste my time. But towering above all was Pandit Shiva Shankar Jha. He was more political than the others, had been a member of the former Legislative Assembly, and if not a Congress man was often mistaken for one. He had greying hair and was in his late fifties. He was a militant and when arguing would put his case with passionate vehemence. Whenever he and Sushil Babu appeared on opposite sides, a battle was truly joined. No two styles of advocacy could be more different, no two lawyers more brilliant. I would often marvel that in this little out-of-the-way town, a young ICS officer, half his age, a product of a wholly different education and from the other side of the world, should be addressed with such respectful and charming formality by one who could almost have been his father, and then treated to such rare intellectual entertainment. When the battle was over, Shiva Shankar would take a little time to unwind, so tigerish had been his effort. I myself would often be a little dazed, and with both sides seemingly unassailably right, I would go reeling back to my bungalow to ponder late into the night which of the two I should back in my judgement.

Out of court, Shiva Shankar would sometimes meet me privately. The fierce militant would then be replaced by a man of saintly sweetness. He lavished affection on me, entered into my problems and difficulties, and with a smiling understanding, tolerated and understood my simple enthusiasms. The fact that his eldest son, Chandra Shekhar, had passed into the ICS and was now in the second of his two probation years in England and had met my future wife in London, gave us a special bond. Because of Shiva Shankar, CS Jha was to become a life-long family friend, but the very fact that the Raj had enabled him to achieve such official parity made its own continuation absurd.

22

6

Madhubani: Neighbours

Across the subdivision, earthen roads wandered from village to village. The bullock carts moved slowly on them, grinding the earth to feathery powder. As they pulled the huge loads, the bullocks sent up a cloud of dust. It hung in the air, settled on paths and houses or drifted over the fields, smudging the young wheat. It was on these roads at intervals of ten to fifteen miles that the European planters had their houses. Sugar was now the all-important crop. Some of the young planters were merely despatchers for the factories. They watched the carts come on to the weighing machines, checked that the clerk recorded the weight correctly, saw the cane hurled off and stacked in railway wagons and then watched the empty cart re-weighed. Once a week they would pay the growers for the cane supplied. Other Europeans were employed at the factory itself. Its iron chimney rose above the trees, a sinister and brutal intruder on the calm and peaceful fields. When the siren blew, it sent the cattle egrets scurrying into the air. Then, when its harsh scream was over, peace would return and the white birds would drift back, settle on the damp patches and preen themselves with jabbing care.

A little to the south of Madhubani lay the bungalow of the Darbhanga Raj, with its massive white pillars, lofty ceilings and vast dark rooms. It housed a European, 'Kiddy' Moore, who collected the rents and supervised the Raj fields. Around his house and those of the planters British social life revolved. Every Saturday, one or other would throw a party and two or three cars would come lurching out over the dusty crumbling roads. It was at these parties that the planters vented their dumb resentment of the country. The visiting wives and daughters sometimes stayed a week or ten days, the men returned to their work.

I had been in Madhubani a fortnight when I decided to visit 'Kiddy' Moore at Pandaul and meet some of my neighbours. It was late afternoon, a feel of drowsy luxury was in the air, and as I drove the twenty miles the light gradually left the land. Soon I was fumbling in the darkness, uncertain of which direction to take. On either side of the road were great bamboo clumps, graceful and mysterious like tall women in long gowns. A little further the dark mango groves were slightly unnerving. Suddenly the car reached a corner and I saw the house ahead. Lights flooded the verandah and a party was in full swing. Kiddy was dancing to a gramophone with the daughter of a sugar-cane manager. She was lush and succulent and as they danced Kiddy patted a curving haunch. 'Mrs Kiddy' looked blandly on. She was fond of her husband and liked his neurotic Irish brilliance. There was nothing to show who I was, but without enquiring my name or business, I was given a drink and asked to sit down. Conversation was going briskly on. Men and women were sitting drinking and in the genial hubbub every one was no one. Among the girls was a slim and sultry character, the orphan daughter of a planter from Muzaffarpur. She was in her early twenties and had the black hair and neat glamour of the Anglo-Indian. She was sleekly smart and exuded a frank and smiling sensuality. She was chatting to a sallow youth from Calcutta - a bank clerk, determined and raffish. They were 'engaged' and Kiddy and Mrs Kiddy were giving them a bedroom for the night. She got up and came over to me 'Are you the new man on the railway?' she asked. 'No', I said, 'I'm only the local Magistrate.' 'Really', she said, 'how interesting', and went back. She did not notice that someone had knocked a glass over and as she resumed her seat she sat down in a pool of gin. It spread across the seat of her slacks. 'Would anyone like to feel it?' she asked.

7

Fire! Fire!

On the west side of Madhubani was a small suburb inhabited by Muslim weavers. They lived in houses with wattled walls and thatched roofs. They set up their looms in the village streets and worked in the open. 'There's one thing I forgot to mention', my predecessor had said as he finished counting the currency notes, weighing the bags of rupees and checking the opium bars in the Treasury as he made over charge to me. 'We've had another fire. It's an almost annual occurrence. Those Muslim weavers will never learn! When a west wind is blowing, the least spark and their whole suburb goes up.' 'What does one do about it?' I asked. 'Oh, give them some relief. They'll build the same sort of huts again. You can't change them.' The news depressed me. I sent for the Vice-Chairman of the Municipality. He was a jovial, energetic Muslim with a down-to-earth manner and a way of humouring people and getting them to do what he wanted. The problem, it seemed, was complicated. The weavers did not want any other kind of dwelling. Why not? Because they could not afford it. He agreed that other people had mud-walled houses with tiled roofs. These did not catch fire easily but they cost more to build. The weavers believed too that their own sort of hut was airier. And another point: huts did not harbour snakes. So what was to be done? I did not want to give them grants of money only to have another fire next year. Moreover, fires of this sort could spread. If the weavers stuck to thatched huts they were jeopardising their own livelihood but even more, they were threatening the whole town. Sixty years earlier, Sir George Grierson - most famous of linguists - had been subdivisional officer in Madhubani when there had been a fearful fire*. Much of the town had been destroyed so he had established a permanent market. It was still there 'Griersonganj' as it was called - but if fires of this sort persisted it might not stay there much longer.

'I think we must make them switch to mud walls and tiles', I said. The Vice-Chairman humouring me smiled. 'It won't be easy' he said. 'But I will

* see note at end of chapter

25

try to talk them round.' He went off and I reflected on what we were in for. Labourers would be needed since without their help the mud walls could not be built. But labourers could be got. It was tiles which were the chief difficulty. Supposing that the weavers agreed, we must have the tiles made before their eyes. If they saw them being made, they would know that all was well. We would not fail them. The Rains were only two months off, but before they came, the houses must be roofed. One point more, I must find the money. It must cost the weavers nothing.

We were lucky. The weavers did not like it but they agreed. The Municipal Overseer marked out the sites for the new houses. Mud walls began to rise. And by good fortune some families of potters agreed to camp in a grove adjoining the suburb, erect their kilns and use the local clay. I left the Vice-Chairman in charge but every week I would walk over to see how things were going. April and May passed. The heat increased but they worked on. As at Arrah, there was a local Charity Fund and I paid for everything from it. It looked as if every weaver would be housed. And then the Monsoon clouds began to gather. A few showers fell. The potters fidgetted. More showers and the grove where they worked swam with water. A lull and the fields began to steam and the kilns could once again be started. We were racing against the clouds. Each morning I would scan the sky. I would ask how many tiles we had. How many more must be made? There was a storm and again the grove flooded. The potters were giving up. I begged them to stay a little longer. There was another lull. The grove dried out. By then we had the minimum stock we needed. We could do with more but we did not need to have them. I pressed the potters to remain. They agreed and then at last the clouds burst. The potters were still there and as the night came on, I could imagine them sitting in the grove, deep pools around them. I decided I must go and see them, so taking my torch, I went out into the rainy blackness. I walked alone along the road. On every side was a raucous din. The bull-frogs were exulting in the rain! I reached the grove and shone my torch. The potters were squatting wretchedly in their little sheds. I told them they could go the next day. They had done magnificent work. There was no point in attempting any more. Let them come to the office early next morning and they would get their wages and a bonus. They salaamed and leaving the sodden grove, I went back through the croaking night. We had won!

*I later wrote to the great linguist Sir George Grierson, a former sub-divisional officer of Madhubani, now a very old man, telling him that the market named after him still existed but that the name had come to be pronounced 'Gilesanganj'. This thrilled Sir

26

George. He wrote back saying 'That word is like a trumpet to an old philological war-horse! For the oldest Indian writers on language noted that the people of Bihar pronounced every 'r' as 'l' and the great Emperor Asoka, who wrote his inscriptions in 250 BC, actually did this. For instance instead of writing 'raja' he wrote 'laja' in the inscriptions set up in the Eastern part of the Ganges Valley. So the Bihar peasants are still conservative! Asoka himself, of course, lived in Patna and was a Bihari.'

Rabindranath Tagore photographed by WGA at Shantiniketan, 1933

8

New Discoveries, Calcutta and Tagore

During the Puja* holidays of 1933 - our September and October - I decided to take a break and go down to Calcutta where I met up with my old Cambridge friend Humayun Kabir, who was now married to Shanti and teaching English and philosophy at Calcutta University. Calcutta proved an exciting and stimulating change from Madhubani. We discussed Indian art and Humayun took me to meet Mukul Dey, the Principal of the Calcutta Art School. It was from him that I learnt more about Kalighat painting. He had written an article on this Calcutta folk art in *Advance* in 1932. I had already seen examples of such paintings in London at the old Indian Museum in Exhibition Road during my year at the School of Oriental Studies, and at that time they had excited me far more than the Indian miniatures on show there. Humayun and Mukul now took me to meet the last of the old Kalighat painters, Nibaran Chandra Ghosh. This old man had ceased to paint but he had a large bundle of old Kalighat paintings in his hut and I was able to buy from him sixteen examples which are now all in the India Office Library (now the Oriental & India Office Collections of the British Library). With their bounding line, and brilliant colour, bold linear rhythm and free watercolour technique, they are a sharp contrast to the delicate art of conventional Indian miniature painting. The subjects were Hindu gods and goddesses, dancing girls, courtesans, snakes, fishes, jackals, prawns and illustrations of the Tarakeswar Case, a scandal which had excited the Calcutta public when in 1873 a Bengali murdered his wife after she had had an affair with the *Mahant* (priest) of the Tarakeswar Temple. The pictures expressed the disgust which orthodox Hindus felt for corrupt contemporary trends. Also in Calcutta I met Ajit Ghose, who had written an article on Kalighat Paintings in 1926.

At this time I was dimly aware that new forces were at work in modern Indian art, but I had been dismayed by the products of the neo-Bengal school which had been fathered by Abanindranath Tagore (nephew of the more

* the nine day festival celebrated by Hindus in honour of Durga and Rama.

famous Rabindranath Tagore) and EB Havell, the Principal of the Calcutta School of Art. These were not modern art as I understood it. I looked for something tougher, more astringent, bolder, something with the vital strength of the village art which I myself, almost by accident, had already come across at Arrah and Madhubani. Mukul now told me that another Indian artist, Jamini Roy, was already working in a modern style based on Kalighat line drawings. It was he himself who had first drawn Jamini's attention to this kind of painting and had urged him to abandon his former academic manner. It was Mukul Dey, too, who had organised an exhibition of Rabindranath Tagore's paintings at the Calcutta School of Art earlier in 1932. The pictures reproduced in his catalogue of the exhibition created a very mixed impression. Some, I thought, were utter rubbish, while others had a wild and vehement originality - something quite different from the weak and feeble pictures which had so far stood for modern painting in Bengal. I felt that here were signs of a break-through, and here, if nowhere else, were the true beginnings of a modern Indian art. I was fortified in this opinion by two of Rabindranath's pictures reproduced that very year (1933) in the *Journal of the Indian Society of Oriental Art*. One was of a veiled face, tall and straight like a *lingam*, the other of a great lumbering monster, bearing a small bird. They were both pictures which aroused my intense excitement and both were obviously modern. Yet there were various hindrances to my liking and understanding. From all the photographs which I had seen of Rabindranath, I had been biased against him by his long hair, his flowing beard, his gentle, effeminate face, perhaps, above all, by the long robe which he constantly wore. These, I felt, were the attributes of a by-gone figure, not at all the cut of a modern artist. And even the English translation of his poetry which had won for him the Nobel prize seemed very remote from the kind of English which I and my generation connected with modern verse. Rabindranath was later to say that his country-men were frankly puzzled by his pictures but I was frankly puzzled by Rabindranath himself. I could not reconcile the public figure of the photographs with the person whose poetry in Bengali had given him so gigantic a stature and whose pictures - the abrupt outpouring of the last four or five years - contained so strange a medley of qualities. I was puzzled and the uncertainty was still there when Humayun Kabir proposed that we should take the train to Bolpur, stay a night or two at Shantiniketan, meet the poet and see his pictures. I was elated at the opportunity and trundling up from the small country station in the morning, I eagerly awaited the meeting. It was, I think, the next morning when I went to see him - a still cool morning after the Rains, the poet sitting outside in an easy chair, his drawing board and inks beside him and to my amazement, a copy of the second volume of a series of essays by different English writers, evaluating various figures in modern English literature. The book was *Scrutinies*, edited by Edgell Rickword, and among the essays was an attack by Peter Quennell on DH Lawrence and his novel, *Lady Chatterley's Lover*. I suspect that Humayun must have told Rabindranath that I wrote poetry for almost immediately we found ourselves discussing problems of obscurity, ambiguity and symbolism in modern poetry. I at once realised that behind that gracious, slightly frail but very majestic figure, there was a mind keenly alive to all that was contemporary in the West. The long saffron robe still distracted me. It was almost too slack for such an agile brain. It resembled a night-gown - the night-gown of a sage. Did it really express Rabindranath's true nature? And then we talked about his pictures. There were portfolios of them in the house. They were the most important thing, he said, which he now wanted to do and sitting in the balmy quiet of that moist October morning, I felt that nothing could be more important for Indian art than that he should go on creating 'the form of things unknown'. A little later he took me into the house and I was shown a series of his pictures mounted and framed on the walls while a quantity of portfolios were brought out, filled with examples of his painting. I also met Nandalal Bose, the modest principal of the local art school, and discussed with him Rabindranath's prodigious production. He told me that it was only in 1928 that the poet had begun, as he said, to 'make lines', welding erasures in his poems into strange new forms. After that he had gone on to follow his fancy, inventing shapes without knowing what they were. Many of his pictures glowed with subtle colours but none of them had conscious subjects and all had sprung up from some hidden source of inspiration. It was these pictures, executed in coloured inks between 1928 and 1930 which Rabindranath had taken with him to Europe and he had been astonished at the impression which they had created in France, Germany and Russia - 'He now does anything', Nandalal Bose told me 'he copies a landscape, a flower or a tree. He tries to do portraits. He borrows books from our art library. He scours books for ideas. He looks at reproductions. There isn't a book on art which he doesn't see.' And I began to realise why it was that the catalogue of pictures at the Calcutta School of Art and even the pictures ranged round his walls were of such uneven calibre. I had, in fact, visited him at a turning point in his career. Two methods were in question. The first was spontaneous and unconscious - the product of forces beyond his rational control. The shapes were tall, angular and often phallic. Sometimes they possessed an angular ferocity and appeared to express some kind of virile defiance. The other method was imitative. Rabindranath had looked at an object or another picture and had crudely copied or adapted it. Such pictures seemed to have no power at all but it was this method which he now appeared to be following. The early pictures were fresh, original and creative. The later pictures were awkward and clumsy. The first were exciting examples of modern art - art which in its methods resembled the work of Paul Klee and even certain pictures by Picasso. The second were notable only for their poor technique. I was amazed that two such different kinds of picture could exist side by side but I knew from my own experience of writing poems that without some kind of inner urge it was impossible to create original art.

Years later, in 1955, when I was writing my book *India and Modern Art*, I began to see Rabindranath's true significance. He himself had always posited a 'magnificent wastefulness' about creative life. It did not seem to matter, then, that so many of his pictures were of no account. His greatness lay in the residue in which, as Nandalal Bose was to say, 'he had broken the ground anew that our future flowers might be more assured of their sap'. In the light of my later studies, I realised that although Rabindranath's early style bore no relation to previous kinds of Indian painting, it in fact unconsciously contained some essential Indian elements - strong, bold outline, glowing colour, aggressive shapes. He had been, in other words 'naturally Indian'. At the same time, he had broken completely with any ideas of naturalistic painting - the kind of art which had been associated with the neo-Bengal school and which stood in such contrast to modern art itself. Yet bold and vigorous though his distortions were they none the less bore some definite relationship to modern India. Rabindranath had not painted political pictures but through their sense of vehement defiance they seemed to express the drive for independence. It was this freedom from previous styles, both Indian and non-Indian, this bold originality, this willingness to create forms in ways which were naturally Indian yet robustly modern which made him the first modern Indian artist; and looking back over the last fifty years I cannot think of any other Indian artist whose influence has been so profound.

9

'Yours in Cow-Service'

'The cow is my mother', the manager solemnly explained as he showed me round the Madhubani *goshala*, the Hindu hospital for sick and ageing cows, and indeed it was like an old people's home. No Hindu would kill a cow any more than he would kill his mother. He might not have the means of feeding it but kill it he would not. As for eating its flesh, that was too awful to contemplate. It would be as if an Englishman ate a favourite cat or dog. So there they were - old cows whom no one else would feed ending their days under cover, munching straw.

To my practical English mind, it was ridiculous, but that was not the point. If you wanted to get on with people, you had to respect their deeply felt beliefs, and in Madhubani, reverence for cows was fundamental. Yet, I wondered, might not *goshalas* be turned to more constructive purposes? By all means collect subscriptions for the aged. Each gift was an act of merit, but what about the future? The local cattle were poor creatures. If the stock could be improved they would more than justify their keep. Stronger cattle meant better agriculture. Why not graft on to each *goshala* a small stud farm? Nandi, the bull, was Shiva's special mount. Install a few good bulls and the ancient institution would begin to trundle into modern times.

I decided I must meet the members of the managing committee and explain my plans. We met and I could see that despite its novelty at least some of them were not against it. I myself, I told them, was devoted to cows. Who could not be? I was not attacking *goshalas*. Far from it. I merely wanted to enlarge their role. Let us give the idea a trial. If they would like some help, I would gladly give it. We could hold a public meeting and I myself would preside.

And so it came about. Meetings were held, subscriptions flowed in and we began by importing a young Tharpakhar bull from the Punjab. It was docile and affectionate, a bull in excelsis. Tharpakhar cattle were famous all over India for their milk and strength. It seemed the very answer to our needs and we celebrated the young bull's arrival by taking it out in procession through the town. A posse of villagers carrying ancient pikes marched ahead. Then came the bull in a flowing red jacket and after it the Committee members and myself riding in cars. The bazaar cheered and through the pandemonium the young bull walked gravely on, the epitome of virile grace. As we went, I recalled the scene in Eisenstein's film, *The General Line*, when the new tractor is paraded. We too were parading something new and there was laughter, jubilation and applause.

Alas! We had counted without the local cows! Our bull was too tall and heavy. We had raced into an experiment without sufficient preparation and knowledge, and the basic facts caught up with us. There was nothing to be done but start again. The young bull, however, was far too marvellous to be sent away. It was a magnificent symbol of our first endeavours. We kept it on for ceremony's sake and when, at the cow-festival of Gopasthami in November, we had our next procession, there he was again, a radiant cynosure, but this time accompanied by three smaller attendants, the best bulls we could get from within Mithila itself.

Some years later when I was posted far away from Madhubani, I was still receiving letters from my old Committee members that began 'Respected sir' and ended 'Yours in cow-service'.

10

Widening Horizons (Puri)

Among the public institutions at Madhubani was the Rohika Central Co-operative Bank. It was a credit organisation that aimed at making cheap money available to the cultivators on the strength of the collective co-operative guarantees. Elsewhere in the province, such banks had often come to nothing. Borrowers had defaulted, bank directors had shrunk from coercive measures. The village societies had wilted and in many cases overdues were now so vast that the borrowers' sureties had had to be sued. The Rohika Bank, however, was a shining exception. It possessed a shrewd and tactful manager and under its Vice-Chairman, Sushil Babu, it had contrived to temper firmness with leniency. As instalments of loans fell due, the societies were in the habit of repaying them and although constant vigilance was necessary, the Bank was thoroughly solvent and the envy of the province.

As Subdivisional Officer, I was *ex-officio* its Chairman, and since the principles of the movement appealed to my ideas of rural betterment, I proclaimed my keenness to support it whenever I could. I quickly saw that as head of the subdivision I had far more power than I appeared to have on paper, and I began to compliment the punctual, to harry the wilful defaulter and to encourage the Bank to organise more societies in other villages.

In these circumstances, when the annual Co-operative Conference came to be held in December, I was one of the ICS officers invited to attend. It was the turn of the neighbouring province, Orissa, to be the location and I learnt with pleasurable excitement that the venue was to be Puri. I should thus be able to visit another province and the journey would count as official duty and be at government expense. What was more, I should be able to see the temple of Jagannath where the great car was taken out each year and pulled with lumbering slowness through a vast and frantic throng. I accordingly wrote to CC Davies, the District Magistrate, saying that I hoped to attend the conference and when I arrived at the station, his car was waiting to take me to his house. The bungalow stood wrapped among the sand dunes close to the sea and as we sat on the verandah, the warm and balmy air and the noise of the breakers induced a sleepy sense of indolent ease.

During the next three days, I sat through session after session, listening to speeches from the delegates as first one and then another resolution was debated. It was here that I first met BB Mukherji and his wife Amala, both from Bihar, later to become our very great friends. But it was the town of Puri itself that I wanted to see, so taking one of Davies's clerks to guide me, I set off one morning on foot. The temple, alas, was a sad disappointment. Its *shikara* or tower was now a gleaming white, its sculptured figures almost invisible beneath a layer of fresh plaster. A visitor was not allowed to go inside, even if one took off one's shoes, and from where I stood, I could see virtually nothing. The image itself was deep inside shielded from prying eyes. I had come in vain, yet almost by accident the day redeemed itself. Wandering through the warm side streets, an Orissan clerk at my side, I suddenly came upon a line of shops displaying pictures of Jagannath. Some were painted on paper, others on varnished cloth, rather like linoleum. They portrayed the god and his brother Balarama, flanking a slim post-like form, their sister, Subhadra. The first examples I saw were infinitely elaborate and cost five rupees each. I bought some. Then I asked if rather poorer ones were available, and leaving the street, we wandered through alleys to a row of hovels on the fringe of the town and there I found some far more primitive paintings. I purchased a pile of old stock and it is this collection which is now in the India Office library. These more primitive paintings provided a fascinating link with the images of Birnath which I had found in Arrah district and suggested that the form of the Jagannath trio had evolved from an earlier and more primitive cult with a wooden deity similar to the Tiger God, Birnath, in Sasaram.

That night as we sat on the verandah drinking whisky, Davies said, 'You can't go back without seeing Konarak. It's the Black Pagoda and it has some of the most erotic sculptures in all India. It's only twenty miles up the coast. You can borrow the car.' I had no idea to what he referred. EB Havell had said nothing about Konarak and even Vincent Smith, whose *History of Fine Art in India and Ceylon* was part of my small library had merely referred to its sculptured horses. Of the erotic or the sensual there was not a word. But Davies's offer was too good to be refused. The car was there and next morning I set off.

As I neared the temple from inland, I saw that its main structure, the tapering *shikara*, had fallen down and now only the *mandap* or porch remained. The temple had been abandoned for many centuries. Either dwindling revenues had led to its neglect and this in turn had caused the collapse or the collapse itself had precipitated the abandonment. No one seemed to know. Yet even in its maimed and bruised state it held the eye. It was a strange gaunt structure, a giant chariot with large stone wheels depicted on the sides. These in themselves were great feats of carving. But it was the sculptures which rose in band upon band up the temple face which made one gasp. Each portrayed ardent couples making love. They were not shown in every pose, for the needs of architecture forced them to appear standing or sitting. Yet short of that, nothing was held back. The figures with their great heads, squat bodies and obvious sex made love with brutal abandon, an animal gusto and vigour, a total acceptance of sex as a kind of boisterous engagement, as if, whether man or woman, each figure had only one compulsive animal need. As a sort of ballet on the act of love, the place swept you off your feet. Its vehement frankness dazed and exhilarated. I wandered over these great, deserted beaches, looking from afar at the grey ruin, a tiny mound under the sky. Then I came nearer and sat down on the sand. And all the time I was filled with a rapturous excitement for which perhaps only DH Lawrence could have found the words. The sculpture was not primitive either in style or in execution but its violent distortion at least linked up with the Puri pictures and the kind of modern art I so enjoyed.

On my way back from Puri I stopped for two days in Calcutta, and it was here shopping in the bazaar that I came across the *Kama Sutra*. I saw a little book that lay for sale on a bookstall: it was intriguingly called *The Hindu Art of Love*, and was by a sage called Vatsyana. It was an English translation from the Sanskrit, but there was something distinctly odd about the translation. It claimed to be by a Mr Gambers, a modern writer, yet the English - the style and spelling - was clearly Victorian. Who was Mr Gambers and what was the *Kama Sutra*? I was to realise much later that Mr Gambers was Sir Richard Burton and FF Arbuthnot, a retired ICS official, their translation plagiarised for cheap Indian sale. I took it back and started to read. And then I had the same amazed thrill which I had got at Konarak. The book was about life in ancient India, an India of about the third century AD. There was a great deal about social life, how courtesans behaved, how kings behaved, how a man-about-town behaved. The book was in seven parts but it was the first two parts which took me aback.

Unlike Calcutta where one often saw women, the Hindu India which I knew in Madhubani was prim and decorous. It was the India of Gandhi, puritanical in outlook, Victorian in its general abhorrence of sex. To Gandhi, sex was bad and the less you thought about it the better. Women led a strangely huddled life. You hardly ever saw them. If you went through a village they quickly veiled their faces and shrank indoors. If you entered a house, there would be a great rush of scampering feet as they made for some inner room. It was only inside doors that the family seemed to exist, and then men always came first. Men sat and ate with men - not with women. Life went on, children were born and reared, but it was all done in what Auden would have called armpit secrecy. Of woman as an active part of life, there was no open trace. But in the *Kama Sutra* woman was there - and not only there but the first thing in life. It assumed that without woman, without sex, life was nothing: and with a strange objective thoroughness, it listed a host of different ways of making love. A man was called a hare, a bull or a horse according to the size of his organ; and in a similar way women were classified as deer, mares or she-elephants. This use of animals as standards of reference had a simple earthy flavour. It seemed to say in words what the sculptures of Konarak had said in stone. For there, on that ruined temple by the sea, it was exactly as if men like bulls and women like mares had all been frantically at one. The Madhubani that I knew was gentle, respectable and polite - a world where women hardly existed. Here was another India where women counted. It was only later when searching for the historical connections that I realised how it had all happened, how this early unrepressed Indian society had given way under the pressure of Muslim rule. It was only later too that I found among the tribal peoples of Chota Nagpur and the Santal Parganas, a world where men and women still had the gaiety and freedom of ancient India.

11

War on Water-Hyacinth

We were being slowly rowed along. With me in the boat were Sushil Babu and the Municipal Overseer. The still water lapped against us. It was a languid, almost stagnant river which wound its way through the town. 'Ah, there's one!' I said and we drew into the bank. The little plant, buoyed up by fleshy floats, had caught in some weeds. It was water-hyacinth and for the last few months I had been mounting a campaign to rid the town of it. I had heard about the plant from Peck when I was in Arrah - the ghastly speed with which it proliferated, the way it choked water channels and covered tanks. Not only did it block progress down the river and pollute the water but its fetid presence in a village threatened health, for it was a breeding ground for malaria. It also reduced the amount of clear water for washing, bathing and watering the cattle. In Orissa Peck had been confronted with mountainous loads of it and as Commissioner he had realised that nothing short of a country-wide onslaught would succeed.

I had seen how prevalent it was in Madhubani and how almost every village tank was infected. The problem was dauntingly vast, but so far as the town was concerned, Sushil Babu as head of the District Board had put the Municipal staff on to it. Every water hyacinth plant, he said, had been pulled up and had now been dumped on the banks to rot. But could we be sure that this was actually the case? Unless every plant had in fact been uprooted, it was bound to return and all the work would be wasted. We plucked the little plant up and moved carefully on. The Rains had broken. The river was full but the early morning air was fresh. It would get very steamy later in the day. It was a Sunday, the courts were closed and we had got up early to avoid the on-coming heat. The Municipality had certainly done its work well. We found another plant some hundred yards on but that was all. So far as the town was concerned, we had won. But a constant watch must be kept or the pest would recur. We landed, tossed the two little plants ashore and made our plans. Once a fortnight the Overseer would take out a boat, cover the whole course and reassess the position. If he found no new plants, we ourselves would wait for a few weeks and then once again see for ourselves.

But how to cope with it in the villages? The District Board was empowered to serve a notice on the villagers, requiring them to clear tanks. But the Board was remote. Its office was in Laheriasarai. None of its officers cared. It was many years since a notice had been served. Pleading with the District Board would be of no avail. The Vice-Chairman would listen in courteous silence. He would see to it, he would say. And then with wry amusement he would watch us depart and put it out of his mind. If anything was to be done, I myself must act. But would it really be worth the effort? I could not possibly cover the whole subdivision. The most I could do would be to inspire some villagers near the town - villages which I could go out to whenever I had time - and trust that once they had hauled the plants ashore, the benefits would be so obvious that they would keep the work of clearance up.

I began with a village four miles away and I took the car as far as possible, left it, and then walked across the fields. It was as well to go in the afternoon since more of the men would be at home. When I arrived, I sent for the headman and told him why I had come. I had a clerk and an orderly with me and both reinforced what I had said. I stood by the tank, gazed at the whole squidgy scene with the dirty green plants - the only lovely thing about them their delicate lilac flowers - and asked the villagers if they liked it. When the floating mass got too voracious, feeble attempts had been made to push it back. But it was like a miniature Sargasso Sea, a waterish island of pneumatic vegetation. The individual could do little against it. It was a tough and thriving menace and like rabbits in Australia, it bred everywhere, defying elimination. The villagers would have to make a joint onslaught and I asked them, then and there, to make it. The request took them aback. They were not prepared for it. It was too rapid, they must have time. But if they started now the work would soon be finished. They could see I was in earnest. I meant all I said. And if they did not start, might they not have me there for hours? Reluctantly, they entered the water. Other men were called and slowly the dripping clumps were pulled ashore. I urged them to tug them up the tank's sides so that none would slip back. It was as if the plants had a sluggish life of their own and given the slightest encouragement would slither back, to breed again. The light ebbed and I strode back to the car. But the next day more work was done and when, a few days later, I went back, the water shone brightly and not a plant was left.

It was a triumph of stern persuasion but it had come off because I was obviously sincere, I was concerned, I desired their welfare and had gone there in person. In three more villages I employed the same tactics and with the same results. I now cited what other villages were doing. If one village could clear its tanks, why could not others? And the more tanks that were cleared, the less chance the water hyacinth would have of reappearing. It was to everyone's interest to stamp it out. Why not get on with it. News of what was happening spread. I began to see that I could safely dispense with a first visit provided I personally inspected each tank later. I therefore sent out notices to all the other villages within the jurisdiction of Madhubani's own Police Station, informing them of what was happening and fixing a date for them also to have cleared their tanks. Tiresome nuisance though it was, they complied. When I inspected the tanks, I could hardly conceal my joyful satisfaction. I praised them for all they had done and begged them to watch out for any new arrivals. If they scotched the water hyacinth plants as soon as they appeared their work would not be wasted. They would have clean and brightly shimmering tanks for years to come. If they did not, all would be lost. They would be back in melancholy squalor, victims of apathy and their own sloth, a prey to a vicious and malignant disease.

The campaign had been encouraging. It had involved, however, a mere thirty villages. Could it be extended? It was only too obvious that alone one could not eradicate water hyacinth completely. Nothing less than a province-wide campaign could do that. Perhaps nothing short of a Water Hyacinth Control Commission could effectively cope with it. Although years later, after Independence, nation-wide efforts for a time eliminated malarial mosquitoes, there was not the slightest chance that the British Raj would embark on so ambitious a scheme. One must be more modest, more humble, more practical.

I debated whether to enlist the support of the local Sub-Inspectors of Police. Mullick the Police Superintendent was unhappy, it would be beyond their proper scope. It might encourage them to neglect their police duties. What would be more absurd if a Sub-Inspector charged with neglecting a dacoity (gang robbery) pleaded absence on 'water hyacinth duty'? No. The police must be left out. There was no obvious agency. I could extend the scope of my notice. I could require more and more villages to clear their tanks. But unless I went myself, I doubted if they would do it. Next year, I would see that none of my local villages relapsed. If I could ensure that their tanks remained free, I would approach the villages in neighbouring police stations. That would take in a good one hundred more villages. Little by little, provided each village took care of itself, water hyacinth would be pressed back. If vigilance had become a habit, if an annual rounding up was accepted, we would have the plague under control. I was contemplating such a strategy when an event took place that put water hyacinth completely out of all our minds.

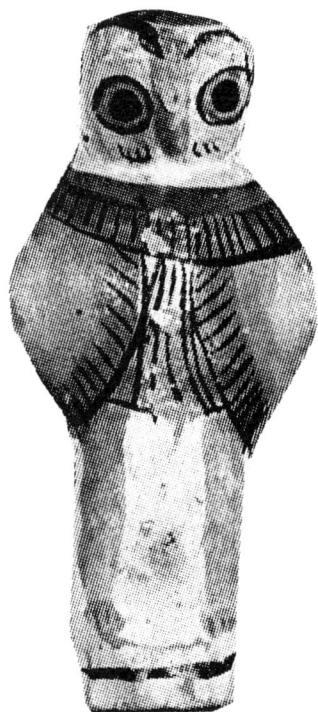

41

12

The Earthquake

On the afternoon of 15 January 1934 I took my seat in court, enquired about the next case and was asked by the pleaders to give them a little time so that the case might be compromised. Their heads were bent over the papers and I waited patiently for the outcome. It was a normal enough day, mild but crisp. I had noticed, however, a peculiar eerie yellow in the sky and as I had walked the hundred or so yards from my bungalow to the court-house, there was an odd hushed silence. The pleaders were still talking together but would not be long they said. Suddenly I heard a low rumbling and felt a slight shiver. The rumbling was like a heavy lorry lurching past or a bus crowded with passengers. I dismissed it as nothing special, but the noise got louder and louder, the dais on which I sat began to lurch and the court-room walls shook. In a flash, the talks broke up, a startled look came over everyone's face, someone shouted 'Bukamp, bukamp' - (it's an earthquake) - and we all dashed for the doors. By then the ground was heaving, everyone stumbled and staggered, great cracks suddenly opened up and the low rumbling became a subdued roar. It was useless to try to stand so I sat down on the ground, wondering for one long moment whether the impossible had happened, the last trump had sounded and the world was about to end. As the shocks threw me about, I pressed my hands down and looked around. The courthouse was still standing but I could see the water in a neighbouring pond surging backwards and forwards, the bottom of the pond bare one moment and covered the next. Some lines by TS Eliot flashed through my mind:

> 'The readers of the *Boston Evening Transcript*
> Sway in the wind like fields of ripe corn'

followed by a verse of AE Housman

> 'These in the day when heaven was falling
> The day when earth's foundations fled
> Followed their mercenary calling
> And took their wages and are dead.'

To sway like fields of ripe corn was grimly funny but what if earth's foundations were indeed fleeing? The ground was trembling under me. It would not take much for a fissure to become a hole or a hole a chasm. If it did, one would be like the damned, irresistibly thrown down into hell... I later learned that it lasted in all three minutes. The shaking, the shuddering stopped, the tremor lessened. We began to pick ourselves up and survey the situation. The court-house itself was standing, a little cracked but otherwise not much damaged. The Treasury was intact. So too was my own bungalow. A bottle of vermouth standing on the mantlepiece had crashed to the ground, but that was all. It looked in fact as if every building that was solidly constructed had survived. But what of the bazaar? I summoned a few assistants and set off. Everyone in court - clerks, pleaders, litigants - had hurried back to their homes and as I went down the main thoroughfares, I met first one and then another of my friends. The scene was one of dreadful, ghastly confusion. Almost every house was down. Here and there a firmly cemented building had survived, but the other shops and dwellings being made of bricks loosely set in mud or of mud alone, lightly plastered, had collapsed as they stood. The tiled roofs had crashed down with them. Dust and rubble lay everywhere and as I picked my way through it, I would find myself looking at a heap of brick-dust only to realise that it was a corpse. How many had been killed I had no idea but as calm gradually returned, and people came to their senses, I realised that the dead and injured were fortunately not as many as had at first seemed probable. The damage was appalling but because the earthquake had happened in the early afternoon in the cold weather, almost everyone had been out of doors and only a few had been trapped inside their houses or struck by falling masonry. I returned from the bazaar and went to my house. Mullick was there and we discussed what to do.

A large tent was already pitched in my compound and we decided that for the present, it would be best if Mullick joined me and we slept inside it on camp beds. I had no idea whether the earthquake was fully over. Little tremors were persisting and if other shocks occurred and we were asleep inside our bungalows, we might well be crushed as we lay. Mullick left at once to confer with the police and find out what had happened outside the town. I myself sent for the municipality officers and began to organise the clearing of the rubble and treatment of the injured. Throughout the afternoon the eerie yellow light persisted but the hushed silence was now over - weirdly broken by conch shells blaring from the temple, to summon sinners, so it seemed, to dread repentance.

The next week disclosed the full seriousness of the situation. Along with Sitamarhi, a neighbouring subdivision in the adjoining district of Muzaffarpur, Madhubani was at the heart of the earthquake [the epicentre, it was officially called]. Almost every road had fissures, bridges were down. The railway track was twisted into strange contortions. In one place the rails had been so squeezed that they formed a figure of eight. Hardly a village had escaped damage. It was not only the houses with their mud walls - some still standing, some cracked, others mere shattered hulks. The wells in many cases had also been affected - their sides had fallen in and who could say where clean drinking water could now be got? Even worse was the sand. This had erupted through the cracks and fissures and had spread out like lava over the fields. Not only must the fissures be filled but the sand itself must somehow be removed. Only the villagers could put such matters right but without the most massive help from Government, the task might well be too much for them.

I decided I must confer with Tony Freston, the District Magistrate in Laheriasarai, so taking the car, following side roads avoiding broken bridges, and where necessary filling in fissures as we went, I eventually reached him late in the evening. He gave me a whisky and we began to talk. Madhubani, it was clear, was the worst affected but other parts of the district had suffered. Not only that - all of North Bihar had experienced shocks. Indeed so vast had been the region affected that even the tall clock-tower of the Secretariat at Patna had swayed and been damaged. The Government had acted immediately. William Brett had been appointed Relief Commissioner and plans were already in hand for mending the railway track, putting up temporary bridges on the main roads and thus restoring mobility. But it was the interior that caused most worry. What sort of help was needed? What help was needed most? We argued late into the night but when I left next morning, we had agreed that as much rice, cloth and blankets as possible should be ferried out for free distribution, small iron tube-wells should be supplied and either cash grants or loans should be made for clearing the sand. The sooner I could give Freston detailed estimates, the quicker the arrangements would be made. I hurried back, summoned Mullick and Sushil Babu and made my plans.

Two courses of action were necessary. Estimates of a sort could easily be obtained from the local sub-Inspectors of Police and these, Mullick assured me, could be got within a week. But it was essential that morale should be restored. The villagers must know that something was being done, that help was on the way, that I cared. I resolved that despite the fissures, I would tour the whole subdivision and show my face. Nothing less would do for only in this way could I discover in depth what had happened. I would also come to know how people were reacting, what they were doing and what they most needed. I could pool their ideas and thus get a better line on what was to be done. By sending word ahead, I could ensure that the roads I would use would somehow be patched up but above all, I must give the villagers new heart. I would talk to them on the spot and urge them to start repairing or rebuilding their houses forthwith. Three days later I started these tours.

The second course of action concerned the town of Madhubani and there I believed I was in a strong position. The work I had done in clearing water hyacinth, my support of the local *goshala*, the aid I had given the Muslim weavers against fire, the friendliness I had for everyone and the informal courtesy I showed all the lawyers had made me well-liked. I was a familiar figure and, as everyone knew, I had the town's interests at heart. With this in mind I broached a drastic new plan. 'Everyone has been complaining', I told Sushil Babu, 'of the narrow roads and all the encroachments. It's almost impossible for a couple of bullock carts to pass in the streets. The Municipality takes no action. Soon there'll hardly be a thoroughfare left. Why don't we make a fresh start? Almost every house has got to be rebuilt. Suppose we make a new alignment and insist that everybody sticks to it. If we make no exceptions, surely in this way, something good will come out of this awful calamity.' 'That is certainly an idea', Sushil Babu said. 'A bit on the revolutionary side but I think we can bring them round.' 'Suppose we form a small group', I said 'We could then go in a body round the town and tell people what we want to do. If I go too, they will know we're in earnest.' 'It's worth trying', Sushil Babu said. And so it came about. The street realignment group included some of the more popular and influential pleaders and even a few shop-keepers. We would go round the town explaining what was in our minds, expostulating with those who objected and finally winning general assent. The Municipal Overseer then marked out the new alignment on the ground and we waited to see what would happen. To my astonishment, everyone began to co-operate - everyone except a single shop-keeper who had encroached on the public road in a very thorough manner. His solidly built verandah still jutted brazenly out a good illegal yard on public ground and nothing we could say would induce him to dismantle it. It had ridden out the earthquake and there it was going to stay. With everyone else co-operating and the whole bar behind me, I had no alternative but to demolish it.

The Chief Secretary later wrote (found recently amongst WGA's papers):

'Patna 24th April 1934
My dear Archer,

I feel impelled, before I go to bed tonight, to tell you, what I thought this morning but said very little of at the time, how much impressed I am at what you have been able to achieve in opening up the roads in Madhubani. I also saw it in Pandaul. Freston tells me you have been equally successful in other towns and villages. I consider it a really remarkable achievement. I do not remember anything of its kind to equal it - to come near it in fact - in nearly 30 years in India. You have undoubtedly done lasting good to the places. To have done it without serious opposition is most unusual.'

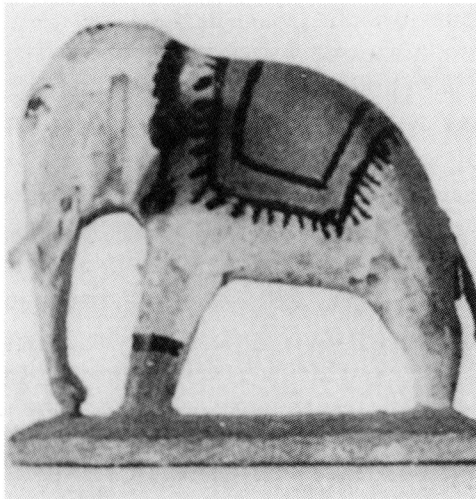

13

I Meet Gandhi

Side by side with the official measures which the Bihar Government was taking, the Congress party had started its own relief organisation. Rajendra Prasad, the provincial leader, opened a Relief Fund and some of the local Congress men began to busy themselves with it. Congress had become once more respectable. Now that the civil disobedience campaign of 1930 had been called off, the gaols gave up their captives and for the first time since my arrival in India, I saw Congress workers in stark white *kurtas* or shirts, their distinctive boat-shaped caps aslant on their heads, mingling freely in the bazaar. None of them had the caged passion of the Bengali Chaturanjan Das. They were mostly very ordinary. But they had all succumbed to the spell of Gandhi. They were not at all hostile to me. Indeed they gladly met and chatted with me as occasion arose. It was merely that along with most Indians they had had enough of the British Raj, and were prepared to defy authority whenever Gandhi asked them to do so.

One afternoon at the end of February, I had got back tired and dusty from a round of villages and after a wash, was drinking a cup of tea beside my tent. Faint tremors still startled us from time to time but they were now much fewer and contained none of the early latent threat. A constable came cycling into the compound and for a moment I took no notice. He lent his machine against the verandah, came towards me, saluted and gave me a slip of paper. To my astonishment it was signed 'Jawaharlal Nehru', and contained the following curt message. 'To the Subdivisional Magistrate. I wish to protest at your insulting behaviour in having me followed by a police officer when I have come here on purely humanitarian business.' Nehru in Madhubani? I had had no inkling of such a visit! None of the local Congress workers had mentioned it. We did not even know that he was in Bihar. I asked the constable if Nehru was still here. No, he had left half an hour ago. How had he come? By car. Where was he going? To Muzaffarpur. I was grieved, shocked, angry, crestfallen and deeply disturbed. Nehru had obviously taken everyone by

47

surprise. He had given no notice. He clearly wanted to see things for himself and it would not have served his purpose if I or Mullick had quietly joined him or had even paid our respects. Indeed the possibility that I might want to pay my respects can hardly have crossed his mind. Most magistrates regarded him as an arch rebel, a fire-brand, a nuisance and unless ordered to meet him, would have kept out of the way. If they had gone to meet him, their actions might have been misunderstood by their superiors. For me he was one of the greatest Indians. I admired his eloquence, bravery and patriotism. I had read his books. I even possessed his tiny pamphlet, *Whither India?* His English reminded me of Bertrand Russell's plain and lucid prose. He wanted India to be free. But what was wrong with that? I also wanted India to be free. It was impossible to have Indian friends in England, Indian colleagues in the ICS, and now in Madhubani, a host of Indians around me, clever, educated, cultured, charming, and still to treat them as unequals, as subjects. How could Nehru have possibly turned on me like this? His action angered me. It was cruel and thoughtless. It could only be due to misunderstanding. And why, without telling me first, had the police followed him? Of course he was annoyed. But why assume that I was responsible? He must surely know that the police did not always take a magistrate's orders. Why turn on me and not on Mullick? And what was Mullick's role in the matter? Did he know of the visit and hadn't told me? Or did he also hear of it only after it was over? I could hardly contain my anger. The note made utter nonsense of all I stood for. It lowered me before the very Indians with whom I worked. I was giving my all to serve them, and now Nehru had brusquely upbraided me. Muzaffarpur was a long way off. It was far more than a hundred miles. But I must somehow put things right. I must have it out with him. If I didn't it would go on rankling. It would foul my attitudes, destroy my admiration. It would do more. It would spoil India for me. It would make me hate Congress, and with a sense of burning grief, I resolved to motor after him through the night.

'Don't do that', Mullick said when he came in. He also had not known that Nehru had been there. He also hadn't had a chance to meet him. Nehru had arrived from nowhere. What else could the police have done? It was no use pretending that Nehru was a nobody, an ordinary person. He wasn't. The police were not snooping when they went along with him. They were only doing their obvious duty. Besides Nehru was known to lose his temper easily and hit people. Suppose he had done so and someone had hit him back? He did not have the sanctity of Gandhi. If he had met with an accident, if there had been a squabble, a brawl, if he had come to any harm, it wouldn't be Nehru who'd have been blamed. It would have been the police. No, the police officer who had followed him had done the only right thing in the circumstances. It was a pity Nehru had blamed me for it. It wasn't my fault. How could it be? And anyway, how was Nehru to know? Why should he have even heard of me? Wasn't I making too much of it all? He hadn't addressed me by name. I was obviously just another British District Officer and he had been annoyed. But he would quickly forget about it. He must have already forgotten about it. What did I think I could gain if I raced after him through the night? I wouldn't catch him before Muzaffarpur. Nehru would be tired. He might even be in bed. Did I seriously propose to burst in on him, show him the note and...

As Mullick spoke, I saw that he was right. My vexation began to ease. What would be gained? Nehru might be moved and touched, but on the other hand, he might not be. If he was not, I would have to return more humiliated than I was now. I would look an even greater fool. Freston, I knew, would understand and because of that I had toyed with the idea of that mad pursuit. Yet, it wouldn't do. Better give it up and with a sense of jangled resignation, I dropped the subject and we talked of other things.

Three weeks later came a very different piece of news. Gandhi was in Bihar and along with Rajendra Babu, he was coming to Madhubani. Unlike Nehru, they would come in public. There would be nothing secretive or private about the visit. They would not expect to see the local officials but they could hardly resent their presence. They would arrive in the morning. Gandhi would address a meeting in the afternoon, hold discussions in the evening and remain for the night. I was determined that this time there should be no muddle. I told a leading Congress man that I wanted to meet Gandhi and Rajendra and have a private talk with them. 'Of course' , he said. 'Leave it to me. I'll arrange it.' The party arrived. For some days previously news had been spreading. A great crowd was there and at four o'clock Gandhi mounted the small rostrum. Mullick and I stood near - not so near as a bodyguard or as a member of the party, but near enough to see him. Gandhi was even smaller than I'd realised. He stood bare-headed, almost bald, with huge steel-rimmed spectacles and large, enormous ears, a thick white wrap round his shoulders, a rucked-up *dhoti* or loin cloth, bare legs and rough shoes. He made no attempt at oratory. He did not raise his voice. He spoke for only five minutes and I doubt if anyone heard a thing he said. The gentle voice said something very slowly, very softly, very firmly. Then he got down from the platform, moved towards the Congress office some forty yards away and was swallowed up. Long after he had gone, villagers were still coming in - not only men but women also, their faces heavily veiled. It was purdah but with a difference. It was like a pilgrimage to a holy place, a bathe in the Ganges, a visit to a temple. Very few of the crowd could have seen him and if they did, they could have had only the merest glimpse. It was enough to have been there, enough even to have been where he had come and gone. They had not had even a sight or a vision yet as they strode away back home, they felt as exalted and comforted as if Rama himself had been among them. 'He will see you and Mr Mullick', a Congress worker told me, 'Come to the ashram at six o'clock.'

As the hour approached, I put on a tie, a clean pair of khaki shorts. I brushed my hair and spruced myself up. Mullick got into his police uniform and gave his brown belt a further polishing. His revolver bulged from its holster, he was looking well turned out. We walked across to the ashram. My Congress friend was there and so was Rajendra Prasad. Rajendra was as tall as Gandhi was small. He wore a *dhoti*, a *kurta* and over it a thick brown waist-coat. He had black hair and a moustache. We had not met previously but I sensed he knew about me. His face beamed with friendliness, and he took me by the arm and led us in. 'This is Mr Archer and Mr Mullick' he said. Gandhi was sitting on the floor at the end of the room, a portable spinning wheel like a tape-recorder before him. He was busy spinning and first said nothing. Two chairs had been set out for us.

The last things we had counted on were chairs and Mullick and I looked at each other. Whatever were we to do? My own impulse was to get down on to the floor as fast as possible, slip off my shoes and sit cross-legged like all the others. It was what I always did in Indian houses. No one in Madhubani would be surprised. But what would Gandhi think? He had thoughtfully had the chairs set out for us. It was a kindly gesture intended to recognise our positions. If no chairs were there, we would either have to stand or sit on the floor. But he was not to know that we would not mind sitting on the floor. We might well have felt insulted or snubbed. This was the last thing Gandhi would have wanted. Then there was Mullick. Dressed as I was, it was easy enough for me to sit on the ground. But Mullick was in full uniform, as if I myself were wearing morning dress. Physically it would not be easy for him. He would feel stiff and awkward. His trousers were tight! And then there was another point. What would the police sub-inspectors and all the constables say? Congress was still their last enemy. They were accustomed to rounding up Congress workers. They had done it in 1930 and they might soon have to do it again. Would they not think it odd if their local Superintendent abased himself in this manner? More than myself, Mullick owed it to them to maintain his dignity, prestige and position. I was in a fix. Mullick I could see, liked the chairs no more than I did and if I sat on the floor, he could hardly do otherwise. Yet he too was obviously disturbed. Whatever he did would be wrong. As an Indian and a patriot, how could he sit on a chair before Gandhi? As a police officer, how could he *not* sit on a chair before him? We had to do something and overcome with embarrassment, we chose the chairs.

As we sat down, Gandhi ceased his spinning. If he had noticed our indecision, he showed no signs of having done so. He looked at me with a benign smile. 'They tell me', he said, 'that you have been doing very good work'. I leaned forward but before I could answer, he took up a piece of cotton, inserted it in the machine. 'We are doing all we can', I answered 'but we are still very short of almost everything'. Whirr, whirr went the machine. 'The Relief Committee will help you. I will ask them to take your advice'. I lent forward again and once more whirr, whirr went the machine. It was as if nothing could be said without a pause. But it was more than that. Spinning was Gandhi's obsession. The spinning machine went with him like a bible. He turned the handle, and as he turned it, it gave him a feeling of calm. There was no fuss, no hurry, no agitation. Slow and punctuated by his machine, our talk proceeded and we touched on most of what I was doing. Tube wells? They are new to the villagers and are always breaking down. If you jerked the pump handle too hard, you damaged the washer. If you damaged the washer, the pump failed to work. It was no good having tube wells unless you had mechanics to look after them. 'All machines are evil' said Gandhi. Clothing? It was now the hot weather. Extra cloth was not needed. 'But *khadi* is', Gandhi observed. 'Without spinning nothing is possible'. Sand? The Government was coping but it would be months before the sand would all be cleared. Myself? I was on the move all the time. The heat sometimes knocked me out but I did not mind. 'You must be careful', Gandhi urged. 'Don't overdo it'. And the earthquake? How and why had it happened? 'Because of sin', said Gandhi.

As the talk went on, it was not his comments that impressed me. Most of them in other circumstances or coming from anyone else, I would have dismissed as childish rubbish, naive and unsophisticated relics of a pre-industrial India. It was rather the way he made them that touched me. He was very, very ugly. Of that there could be no doubt. But he radiated love. His smile exuded sympathy, understanding, appreciation, and above all loving concern. His charm magnetised and once you had experienced it, you succumbed. You were his for life. When at last we took our leave, Mullick and I were both too moved to say a thing.

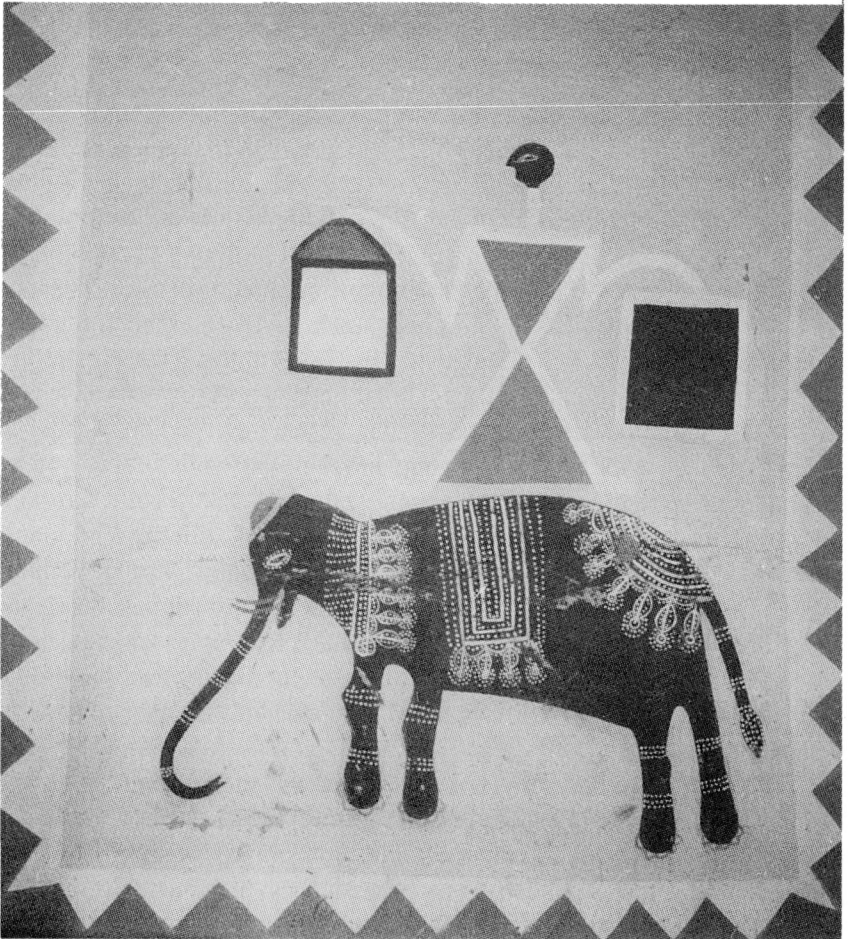

mural

14

'Into Hidden Maithila'

During the nine months which preceded the earthquake of January 1934 I had been to every part of the subdivision, inspecting a dispensary here, a police station there, and striving to find out what irked the local people. I had done this as part of my own education because I believed that a Subdivisional Officer must above all know his subdivision. I had been earnest but not wholly earnest for in an area which even more than Shahabad was full of local godlings, little shrines and ancient practices, there was much to beguile the eye, tease or enliven the imagination and arouse one's curiosity. I had ridden out one evening to a village close to Madhubani itself and chanced upon a small white temple. The *mahant* was there and dismounting from my horse, I stopped to have a chat. He invited me to see the image. I took off my shoes, went up the steps and peered inside. It was a black stone dressed in doll-like clothes. Only the *mahant* could handle it but when he did, he told me, it was 'warm and soft like flesh'.

Another day, a boy, Kalu, had taken me out to his father's home in Sakri. The occasion was the festival of Kali and a splendid image of the goddess standing on her spouse, had been put up. Kalu's father told me 'We don't believe that this is Kali herself, but it makes her real in our minds and it helps others'. As I looked at the villagers staring at the image, it was as if I was back in the thirteenth or fourteenth century in Europe and was watching peasants staring at a Black Madonna. A little later the puja would be finally consummated with the beheading of seven goats, but I did not stay for that!

On yet another occasion, this time in early November, I had motored through the mango groves and bamboo clumps to Madhepur, a village twenty-five miles to the south-east. An orange sunset imbued the evening with placid calm and along the horizon the snows stood sharply out. The air grew cold and suddenly I came upon an immersion ceremony taking place at the Kamla River. An image of the goddess Bhagavati in a small reredos was poised on some planks which in turn had been put across a boat. An old

Maithil Brahmin lady - the patron of the ceremony - was doing a furtive purdah puja from inside a palanquin and on the bridge and banks, the villagers had crowded. Banners were waving gently in the evening air and in the sky fireworks cascaded. The boat was pushed off, taken down stream, manoeuvred across the river, brought up-stream and then poled back. As the fireworks spurted in the water, I felt as if I were standing on the smooth mud of the Styx and the boatman was Charon. At times the boat looked like a burning barge and against the falling sparks the boatmen stood like charred skeletons. People were standing in the water and the moonlight flickered on the wobbling surface. I looked at the sky, the fire balloons fraily floating, and at the shore with the great banners magnificent in the fading light, and as I stood I sniffed the fireworks like incense.

Such experiences had taught me that however pressing my business, I could ill afford not to stand and stare. I was none the less, quite unprepared when, after the earthquake, I went to Benipatti to assess the damage. The houses with their mud walls had been severely damaged yet not so damaged that none were standing. I could see beyond the courtyards into some of the inner rooms and what I saw in the house of a Maithil Brahmin took my breath away. In normal times I would never have seen them since the rooms were private and intimate. But now they stood exposed and with astonished eyes, I saw that the walls were covered with brilliantly painted murals. Bright yellow, green and magenta gave them a frail and flickering majesty and among the yawning cracks they stood out with radiant glory. What I was seeing was a marriage chamber, a *kohbar*. It was here that the bride and bridegroom would be espoused and everything painted was designed to bring them prosperity, good fortune and fertility. There were figures of the bride herself and other ladies, of gods and goddesses, Krishna, Radha, Durga and parrots - the love-birds of poetry - while covering a whole wall was a forest of lotuses, a symbol of fertility, the flowers pierced with a thick phallic pole. The house belonged to a Maithil Brahmin. Everything meandered, yet everything cohered. The faces had a gay insouciance, the fanciful contortions of a Klee or Miro. The figures also had a dream-like vacuousness. Their very freedom from what was normal sparked off the imagination and one felt as if one was in a fairy-like palace, brimful of wonder. Since stumbling on the stone images of Birnath on that early tour for tiger in Shahabad, I had seen nothing which so instinctively took for granted the assumptions of modern European art.

I wandered further down the village. Almost every house had murals, some hopelessly battered and broken, others unaffected. Every Maithil house

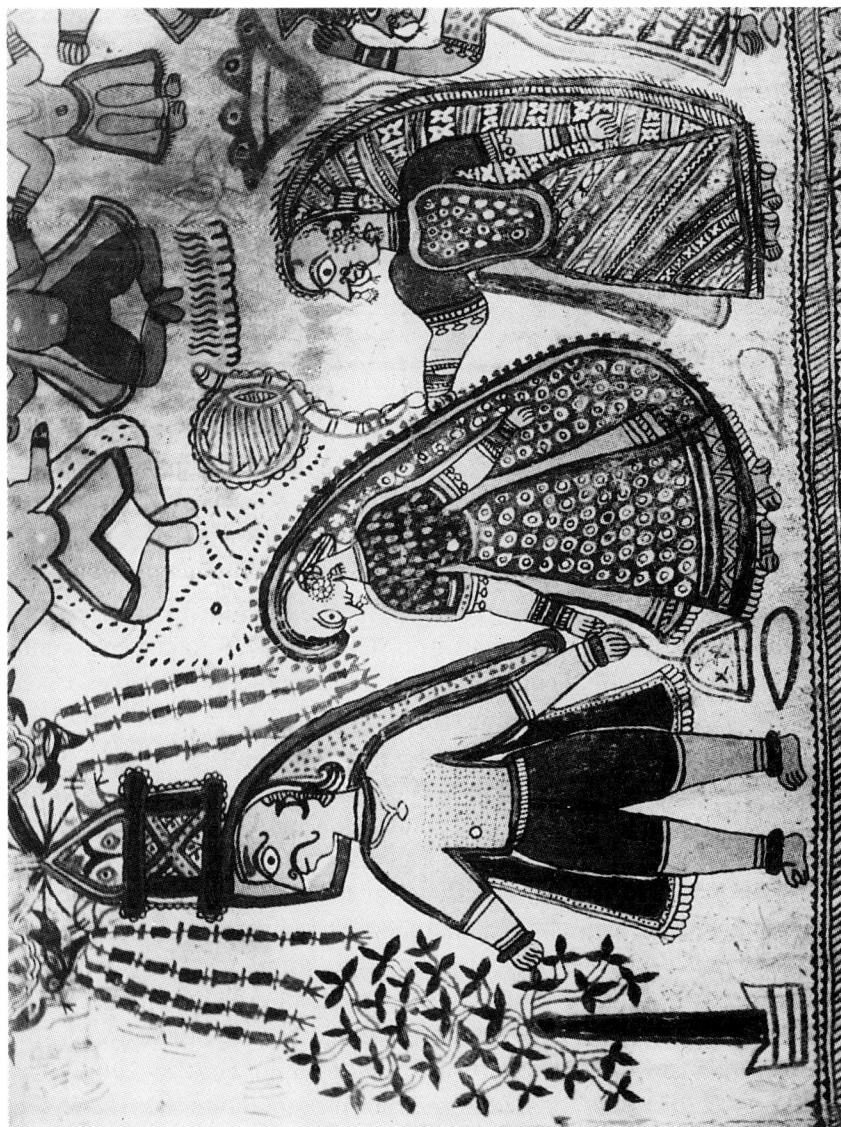

Bride and bridegroom with attendants (mural, Maithil Kayash, Darbhanga)

employed roughly the same conventions, the same fey wandering lines, the same injection of faces with doll-like innocence. Every girl, I was told, was taught how to paint these murals and when she went to her husband's house she took her skill with her. All murals were the work of women. Men had no part in them. In a kind of underground conspiratorial manner, a sort of freemasonry of the arts, each group of women tapped a regional reservoir of idioms providing each bride and bridegroom with the heavenly images requisite for their bliss. On only one other occasion, they said, were special murals painted. It was when a boy had reached puberty and was ripe for receiving his sacred thread. Then too it was necessary to associate with him everything that was auspicious and while the love-birds might disappear, the same benign deities would be evoked in meandering lines and gay and winsome colours.

Besides Brahmins, Kayasths also followed the same age-old Maithil tradition. They too covered the walls of the *kohbar* with arresting imagery and they too supplied the adolescent with every aid to caste manhood. But the style of their murals was quite distinct. It presupposed the same liberties, the same repudiation of truth to natural appearances, the same determination to project a forceful idea of a subject rather than a factual record. But in contrast to Brahmins, Kayasth women were vehement. They portrayed their main subjects with shrill boldness, with savage forcefulness. Not for them the frail and whimsical fancies of a floating world. They were not so keen on colour and in some cases the entire wall was covered with compositions all executed in a blood-like madder. In one house, I was astonished to see a figure of a bride, her veil a robust triangle, her face a single huge eye. If Maithil Brahmin murals resembled Miro or Klee, here was Picasso naked and unashamed. And then, as if to emphasise their caste differences, Kayasth women filled every vacant space with something - little figures, odd patterns, and niggling, needling strokes. I had already sensed that Brahmins and Kayasths were fundamentally different in temperament and makeup. Brahmins were priestly, Kayasths were clerkly, but nowhere were these differences plainer than in these secret murals, fondly produced from generation to generation by the women of each family and now suddenly exposed to alien British eyes by the calamity which had struck us all.

I must confess that for at least an hour, I forgot the earthquake and its horrors. I was entranced by what I saw. It gave me a new vision of Mithila. I felt myself modern. I liked modern art. They were medieval in attitude. I was stridently contemporary. They were products of pre-industrial India. I was a

Veiled bride (mural, Maithil Kayash, Darbhanga)

57

product of sophisticated England. Yet in these murals we somehow electrically met. What they took for granted, I considered superb. They were unconscious, I was conscious. But whether deliberate or accidental, the art was there and it made us one. I had never felt myself so much a Maithil as on that day when faced with shattered walls, I saw the beauty on the mud.

Later when I became Collector of Purnea District in 1937-38, I discovered that this type of wall painting spread into the eastern side of this adjoining district. When I was Provincial Census Superintendent in 1940 I was able to make a careful study of Maithil painting over a wider area. I took photographs of the murals in situ and collected some of the womens' aide-memoires on paper which each family preserved. In 1949 I published an article on the subject in *Marg*. Mrs Pupul Jayakar of the All India Handicrafts Board, New Delhi, happened to read this article and paid a casual visit to the area in the late 50s, but in 1966-67 when Bihar was struck by famine and the Indian Government was considering how to give relief in a practical way, she recalled my article and wrote to me asking for the names of the villages where I had seen the paintings. She then visited this area and started a relief project in the villages of Jitwarpur and Ranthi. As part of the project she encouraged some of the old ladies to paint on paper the designs they knew so well. She eventually found about 20 outstanding painters. She gave them large sheets of strong paper and poster paints and persuaded them to make paintings which she could sell at the Tourist Board in New Delhi. They proved a great success. Later she arranged for some of these women to paint the walls in the new hotels that were springing up in Delhi. As many visitors to India now know, these 'Madhubani Paintings' have proved a tremendous success and they are still being marketed. Inevitably this mass-production has led to a decline in quality, but the confidence that the women have now gained has released reserves of hitherto unconscious imagery.

15

The Voyage Out

As a result of all this arduous relief work which Bill continued to do throughout the hot weather of 1934, he collapsed with heat-stroke and was invalided home in May. I came down from Oxford at the end of the summer term and we were married on 14 July 1934. Bill soon recovered after a brief holiday and we sailed for India on board the P & O liner, SS NALDERA on 28 September 1934. Apart from short holidays in Switzerland and Germany, I had not travelled widely and the voyage proved a fascinating experience. These voyages have been described over and over again in 19th century journals, but as a result of modern air travel they have now become a part of British social history.

The first part of the voyage was unromantic and very rough, especially in the Bay of Biscay. The sky and the sea were cold and gloomy but as soon as we reached the Mediterranean everything changed, and the voyage became sheer delight. Tangiers, its white minarets silhouetted against dark cypresses, soon came in view and we went on shore. The town with its white houses was like the background of an Italian primitive. We wandered up and down steep streets, the houses brilliant with blue morning-glory and purple bougainvillea. Then the boat docked at Marseilles for several days as many passengers from England bound for India preferred to shorten the voyage by joining the boat there, having crossed France on the Blue Train, rather than sailing from London as we had done. Two or three hundred new passengers came on board there. During this break Bill and I made an excursion to Avignon. I had never been to Southern France and it was a delight to see the countryside painted by Cezanne and Van Gogh, artists whom we greatly admired. We rejoined the boat and the voyage through the Mediterranean was delightfully warm and sunny. I enjoyed watching the flying fish and dolphins that accompanied the boat. At Malta we went on shore again and explored Valetta with its steep steps and fine Baroque churches. At Port Said we bought topis at Simon Artz and watched the 'gully-gully men' with their sleight of hand tricks. We had a strange experience in the Suez Canal as a thick mist engulfed us and the pilot made an unusual error - the boat stuck on a sandbank in the Bitter Lake. There was uproarious chaff as other boats speeded past us, the passengers leaning over the rails jeering and laughing. But there was consternation too for we were carrying many brides-to-be, the times of whose weddings in Bombay had already been fixed and a Captain is fined for every hour he is late. Eventually tugs and a lighter came to our rescue from Aden. The first attempt to haul us off failed. Baggage then had to be unloaded until we were again afloat, and everyone then relaxed. At Aden we had a delightful swim. A beach had been cordoned off with wire-netting to keep out the sharks, the water was so clear that as we swam, we could see little striped fish darting around and beautiful shells in the sand below. The ship gradually caught up time crossing the Indian Ocean and in the end we were only two hours late in Bombay.

Mildred at Ranchi, 1934

Although I had greatly enjoyed the voyage from the point of view of the sea and the scenery, I was less happy about the people I had met on board. They were quite unlike any I had known in England. They fell into distinct groups who barely mixed - civil servants, army men, planters and business men. I felt many of them, especially the women, were all playing a part pretending to be what they were not in England. As a newly-wed, numerous memsahibs gave me advice about life in India. The wives of civil servants stressed the importance of etiquette at dinner parties - the need to consult 'the book' for correct seating at table, the need to constantly inspect the kitchen and watch the issue of foodstuffs for 'no servant could be trusted'. There was constant talk of the Club and bridge. Nothing ever seemed to be said about India or Indians apart from servants. On the other hand I found many of the men most interesting - there was Sir Stewart Macpherson, a High Court Judge at Patna, George Fawcus, the Director of Public Instruction in Bihar, and Mr Spiller, Headmaster of the *Zillah* School at Ranchi, all of whom I particularly enjoyed talking to. Many of them teased me for my 'left-wing' views and said they would be interested to see how long these would last once I settled down in India!

On arriving at Bombay on 22 October, Bill's old bearer, Adwardhan Khan, was patiently waiting for us on the dockside. He immediately collected our luggage, and efficiently took over all the arrangements, salaaming me in a most reverential manner! He must have been apprehensive wondering what the new memsahib was going to be like. Bill reported his arrival to Government and discovered that he had been appointed as Subdivisional Officer of Gumla, an aboriginal area in South Bihar. We also sent a telegram to my brother in Bengal alerting him to our arrival. Before leaving Bombay we had a quick drive around the city, along the sea-front and past the fine mansions on Malabar Hill. We then caught a train to Chakradapur, a journey which was itself a new experience. I was greatly impressed by the bearer who appeared with meals as if by magic and made up our sleeping bunks with quiet efficiency at night. Bill's old car and driver, Iltaf, were waiting for us at Chakradapur and we then drove to Ranchi in Bihar where Bill reported his arrival and contacted the Deputy Commissioner, Mr Merriman, under whom he was to serve. My brother in Bengal, also of the Indian Civil Service, who had been Bill's friend at Cambridge, and whom I had not seen for three years, was also waiting to welcome us and we at once settled down to discussing family news.

16

Gumla, Initiation

The next day we set off for Gumla, about 70 miles from Ranchi. I could not have started my married life in a more delightful area. Although Gumla was the headquarters of a subdivision of Ranchi District in Chota Nagpur, it was little more than a village. On arriving we found that the out-going Subdivisional Officer, Rai Sahib Jag Dutt, was still in residence and had not yet packed up, so we decided to go off to Madhubani in North Bihar to collect Bill's belongings which had been left there when he went on leave.

This trip gave me a good feel for the province with the change from the hills and forests of Chota Nagpur to the flat paddy fields of North Bihar. After crossing the Ganges we stopped at Sonepur, where a great fair was being held on the north bank. This famous fair is held every five years in October and November. Hindus believe that it commemorates a great fight between a huge crocodile and Gagendra, Lord of the Elephants. Crowds of villagers make their way there, some to purchase agricultural tools and household goods, most just to enjoy the fun. For the British officers and planters in North Bihar it was a chance to meet each other and relax. Great tents had been erected, polo matches and races were being held, but by the 1930s, the Fair was less lavish and more educational than it had been in the 19th and early 20th centuries. The Agricultural Department now used it to give publicity to new breeds of cattle and new agricultural implements. For the local officials, the organisation of the Fair was a formidable task; for the surrounding villagers, it was a break from their monotonous routine and a chance to see lumbering elephants, cantering horses and fine cattle.

Today these things have changed. I noticed, during a return visit to India in 1989, a newspaper article in the *Searchlight* on the Fair: 'Affluent Bihar has now devised entertainments that lie nearer to contemporary ostentatious tastes. The first main attraction now lies in the night cabaret tents where prosperous peasants from Chapra and Purnea buy ten rupee tickets to watch 'Miss Krishan' or 'Miss Usha' peel off gold sheath evening gowns and elbow-length black gloves to reveal scanty bikinis. The strip-tease artists are of a certain age but blanket-draped villagers watch in gratified silence while they gyrate and gesticulate more suggestively than any Paris floor show. This clearly is progress! It is difficult as the noisy pageant of this gathering on the north bank of the Ganges unfolds to accept the Chief Minister's claim that 600 million acres in North Bihar are annually inundated, that this year's damage stands at a colossal 6,000 million rupees, that 13 million people were hit by the floods while 15,000 houses were washed away. The tawdry magnificence of the Sonepur mela, its original religious and agricultural *raison d'etre* lost in the glittering illuminations of cabaret, nautch shows and exhibitions, a giant circus and a multitude of restaurants, is untinged with any sense of grief.' My main memory of the Fair in 1934 was of its huge size, the vast crowd of villagers and the dense pall of smoke from the cooking-fires which descended over the whole area in the evenings so that everyone was red-eyed, coughing and weeping!

The next day we drove to Madhubani. Bill's old office staff and a crowd of local people were patiently waiting to receive us and even his bulls, wearing colourful jackets, were lined up to greet us! We collected Bill's boxes and trunks, arranged for the larger pieces to be despatched by rail and then set off back as quickly as possible, for Bill, although sad to leave his former subdivision, was keen to get settled at Gumla. Back there, he quickly took over charge and his predecessor left. Bill already loved the area from his Settlement days, with its hills and pre-Dravidian tribal people and I was keen to get settled in my first Indian home.

Our house in Gumla was a tiny brick bungalow with a verandah front and back. We had no electricity, no telephone and no sanitation. The sitting room with its two French windows opened on to a front verandah and two arches at the back of the room opened into the dining room behind. This in turn led through two French windows on to the back verandah with its pantry and store cupboards. There was only one bedroom, but two tiny dressing rooms and bathrooms complete with tin tubs, large earthenware pots of water and wooden 'thunder-boxes'. Rai Sahib had still not moved out so when we arrived we camped in the Circuit House next door for a few days. This was a pleasant building standing in a garden bright with pink and white oleanders and yellow cosmos. As soon as Rai Sahib had left, we went to explore our future home. My heart sank, for the whitewashed walls were stained and green, cobwebs everywhere, and lumps of sacking hanging in all the open doorways (for Rai Sahib's wife was in purdah). Fortunately the Public Works

Department soon arrived and redecorated the whole house until it was shining white throughout.

Our Marshall trunks had by now arrived from Bombay and the boxes we had brought back from Madhubani were waiting, so we moved in. I was most excited to get unpacked. I longed to arrange the things we had brought out with us, including our wedding presents. There were five large reproductions of modern paintings - Van Gogh's 'White Roses', Cezanne's 'Mont St Victoire', Matisse's 'Odalisque' and 'Gold Fish Bowl' and Chagall's 'Circus Rider'. We had also brought out with us Susie Cooper china and Swedish glass. Fortunately there were scarcely any breakages, in fact most of the glass and china is still being used by me today. I was intrigued by the lizards which scampered round the walls and shed their tails if anyone attempted to touch them. We soon gave them names for they became permanent, if uninvited, guests.

Like the house, the garden had been badly neglected, but a young Christian *mali* (gardener) named Raphael, soon cleared it for us and some fine trees and plants emerged from the tangled undergrowth. There was a custard-apple tree beside the house which eventually produced the creamiest fruit I ever tasted in India. In one corner of the garden was a giant *sisam* tree where I was later to watch an exciting fight between a family of *mynah* birds and a huge *daman* snake that was raiding their nest. Opposite the front verandah was a silver-oak tree where a yellow white-eye had its tiny nest. There were numerous neglected rose-bushes which after pruning produced lovely white blossoms tinged with pink. In the garden at the back to the right of the bungalow was the cook-house and a line of servants' quarters. On the left was a wicket-gate leading to Bill's office and court and to a large grassy area with a hockey pitch and tennis court where according to the season we exercised regularly.

Behind the house and garden was another open green expanse leading to the gaol. Here were a number of *kachinar* trees laden in season with pink and mauve blossom. In front, the garden was bordered by a high hedge behind which lay a road leading up to the hills along which once a day the post-runner passed carrying his postbag on a spear over his shoulder with a bell that tinkled as he ran. So regular was he that we could set our watches by him! The road led to villages in the nearby hills and on market days Uraon villagers would pass by in groups chattering and singing as they returned to their homes. In the opposite direction, the main road was bordered with the houses of the pleaders and led to the bazaar. There was a tank nearby in which every year, at the time of the *Chait* festival, the local women wearing yellow saris would stand at sunset with the water up to their armpits, chanting their prayers and making offerings of fruit and flowers. The men watched from the banks and the children rushed around flying their kites.

I was thrilled by the new varieties of birds, flowers and trees that I saw. As the hot weather approached the bird cries changed. The 'copper-smith' beat out its regular note and the koel's cry rose higher and higher. The blue-jay, the green barbet, the bulbul and the dull seven sisters all frequented our garden. Purple sunbirds hovered over the red and salmonpink hibiscus blossoms near the verandah. On our evening walks we saw snipe, green parakeets and the white paddy-birds which strutted in the rice fields. The trees were constantly changing with the season. As it grew hotter the dark gnarled branches of the *frangipani* tree suddenly produced their waxen blossoms, the mauve jacaranda and the scarlet-orange gold mohur burst into flower. The *palas*, the 'Flame of the Forest', with its twisted branches, produced its brilliant red parrot-beaked flowers with their black calyxes. The *simal* tree, with its silver-grey trunk, dropped its red waxen blossoms on to the grass.

One of the great delights of the cold weather, which followed the Rains, was touring on foot throughout the district for several weeks on end and camping with tents from December to March. We walked from one camp site to another. We took with us two sets of tents - one of which was erected for the first night's stay and the second was sent on ahead to the next halting place, and so on. By the time we arrived at our first camp site the tent had already been pitched, as well as a smaller one for the cook and the servants. The villagers, who had been alerted to our arrival had already gathered waiting to meet Bill and discuss their problems. In the evening, as it grew dark, a great bonfire would be lit, around which we all sat. After all the local problems had been discussed with Bill, he would persuade the villagers to dance and sing for us. It was on these tours that he collected the Uraon and Santal poems which he later published in *The Blue Grove* (1946) and *The Hill of Flutes* (1974).

Today things have greatly changed. Few officers tour on foot with tents but drive by car along *puckha* roads and stay at the local *dak* bungalows. In 1934 the old custom still persisted and I am sure it led to a more intimate knowledge of the countryside and of the villagers' problems.

Nearly every evening in the cold weather, when we were not out on tour, we played tennis with the pleaders. We were a comic collection. There was Mohan Babu, with his steady lobbing. He was a sensitive cultured Bihari who played in his long neatly pleated *dhoti*, his socks kept up with suspenders. There was his stocky brother, Gokul Babu, the most successful of the town's lawyers. There was 'Batcha Babu', a jolly plump young pleader who dashed about the court, 'Potol', a young Bengali pleader, was an excellent player, but Mandaraj was our starturn. This stylish young Deputy Magistrate sported white trousers with a knife-edge crease, a navy blue beret and doeskin shoes. He always arrived with two racquets! There was also the other Deputy Magistrate, Daniel Lakra, a kind dumpy young Christian Uraon wearing a *dhoti*. Our games were the craziest fun with delightful naked little Uraon ball-boys rushing around. Gradually I came to know the families of these pleaders and visited their wives. There was only one Muslim pleader, a Mr Zafar, with a young purdah wife who always shrank behind the end of her sari when I visited her; the rest were all Hindus. I soon came to love the slow rhythm of life in Gumla, so different from the restlessness of London.

During the rainy season when at headquarters, we played hockey every evening with the school-boys. The game had been introduced by the Jesuit missionaries. This was even crazier than the tennis as the pitch was extremely rough. I played on the wing and Bill played in goal, holding an umbrella over his head until he saw the ball approaching. But I loved the Rains for the whole countryside suddenly burst into dazzling green.

I had no sooner got unpacked, the bungalow straight and our books shelved than we had to vacate it. One morning I was sitting talking to Daniel Lakra when a little brown insect fell on to the arm of my chair. 'What is the Hindi name of this little insect?' I asked, endeavouring to show my interest in Indian natural history. There was a pause. 'Madam', replied Daniel solemnly, 'It is a bug.' I had never seen one before. Close examination by the Public Works Department (PWD) soon revealed that the beams of the ceiling, the skirting boards and the shutters were alive with these unwelcome guests, a legacy from our predecessor. We were ordered to move into the Circuit House next door while they sealed and fumigated the house. We then moved back and had no further trouble.

In the evenings if we were not playing tennis or hockey, we went on long walks through the neighbouring villages and paddy fields and watched the changing agricultural routines - the ploughing of the fields, the sowing and transplanting of the paddy seedlings, the reaping, threshing and storing of the harvest. On these walks we went into the village houses and chatted to the occupants, admired their babies and listened to their problems. We saw the women gathering the fallen *mahua* flowers for making spirit and heard stories of how they were sometimes mauled by the bears who particularly relished the blossoms. It was in Gumla I first saw the 'bachelors' dormitories' where the young men until marriage spent their evenings and nights. It was in Ranchi too that we first met the old anthropologist Sarat Chandra Roy who for many years had edited *Man in India*, the anthropological journal which Bill and Verrier Elwin were to edit a few years later after Mr. Roy's death.

In Gumla I was able to become aware of the rhythm of the changing agricultural routines without any social distractions. The surrounding countryside was most beautiful with its *sal* forests, the shiny leaves showing pink in the spring, and the red-soiled uplands golden with *surguja*, a small sunflower cultivated for oil. Sadly the forests were rapidly being felled for timber and serious erosion was taking place. One of Bill's main official concerns at this time was the preservation of the forests which in theory were protected but which in practice were often being illegally felled by the landowners, contractors and villagers.

This quiet immersion in the changing seasons and the agricultural routine was one of the joys which it would have been difficult to savour if Bill had been posted to a larger and busier town, or had been in the Secretariat, with its constant round of official social life. I was indeed fortunate in my initiation into India and it is these delightful memories that still linger more than 60 years later.

It was clear that the first thing I must do was to learn Hindi, so every morning before office hours, Daniel Lakra, and later Mohan Babu came to the bungalow to teach me. I gradually learnt the script and after mastering a primer, moved on to read a child's version of the *Ramayana*. I later used some of Bill's probation-year text-books.

I never felt lonely or isolated as we had frequent visits from touring officers who usually stayed at the Circuit House next door and came to us for meals. There were visits from the Deputy Commissioner, Mr Merriman, on his inspection tours, the Deputy Inspector General of Police, Public Works Department officers, Forest Officers and School Inspectors as well as Mr Peppe, the manager of the estates of the Maharaja of Chota Nagpur. He was a great character, descended from a long line of country-born Europeans. I had violent arguments with him as he was a Tory of Tories! Through these visits, I gradually began to understand the administrative structure of the District and the different types of work that were being done. There was a Roman Catholic Mission nearby with Jesuit priests from Louvain. They were highly efficient and well-educated. They frequently called on us bringing me small gifts of fruit or eggs - on one occasion a clutch of turkey-eggs which unfortunately failed to hatch out. Sometimes when they came to dinner, they would bring with them a bottle of unconsecrated communion wine - 'exempte de toutes poursuites judiciaires' they explained! One old Jesuit, Father Cardon, who lived in the nearby subdivision of Simdega, also sometimes came and visited us. He had an encyclopaedic knowledge of Indian plants and was a great gardener. He smoked a cheroot continuously and his flock firmly believed that this was a necessary form of *puja* to his God!

But most exciting of all our neighbours were the Uraons of the nearby villages. Soon after we moved into the bungalow, we heard distant singing at night and the sound of flutes and drums. Bill knew from his days in Settlement in 1932 that the Uraons were fond of dancing and singing. But now he was curious to know *what* they were singing. So we would get out of bed, dress and taking our torches quickly steal out into the adjoining fields and watch the dancing - the girls in long lines with their arms interlocked, wheeling, gliding and swaying in ever-changing patterns, while the boys, with flowers behind their ears, gambolled around them, drumming, singing and fluting. On a moon-lit night it was a magical and unforgettable experience. With his interest in vernacular poetry, Bill was curious to know more about the songs they were singing and this led him to start learning Uraon himself and organising the collection of the songs. We began to attend village ceremonies such as marriages and marriage negotiations. Gradually the symbolism of the poetry became clear - birds and animals such as bears and doves or fish symbolised the boys and girls

'South of Bassia
In the twin tanks
A fish is living
No, it is not a fish,
It is the bride selected by the mother,
The bride chosen by the father.'

'From the clear springs the water flows,
Water that the doves sip and the pigeons drink,
In pairs they have come, the wild geese,
In pairs they have come,
No, it is not the wild geese,
It is the girl the elder brother chose.'

The use of such symbolism provided a refined method of discussing matters that could otherwise be embarrassing for the families. Dowries and marriages could be arranged and negotiated in a much more delicate manner through the use of symbolism and poetry. The girl's party, for example, would arrive at the boy's house and announce that they owned a fine marrow on which they had spent much care, watering it, tending it until it had become a most beautiful specimen. How much would the boy's family be prepared to pay for this fine vegetable? Other songs were sung to ease tiring and monotonous work such as transplanting paddy-seedlings or pounding rice. Their whole life was in this way interspersed with poetry and song. When we went on leave in 1939, Bill submitted translations of a number of these poems which he had collected to Allen and Unwin, who published them in 1940 as *The Blue Grove*.

Throughout the cold season we toured continuously, often with Mr Subhawal, the Conservator of Forests, a fine strong Punjabi who organised the demarcation of the 'coups' which could be felled in rotation, thus giving other areas of the forest time to recover. These marches during the cold weather with the scent of the yellow-green *sal* blossom in the air, were a great delight.

We would go out on tour for several weeks at a time, walking from village to village and camping in large 'cottage' tents. There were separate small tents for the servants, for the cookhouse and for the latrines. The floor of our large main tent was covered with straw, on top of which a blue-striped cotton *durrie* was spread. The tent had a small section at the back for a bathroom and a porch in the front where Bill had a table and would sit dealing with the files which came out daily from Gumla by runner, settling legal cases on the spot or discussing problems with the villagers who would come and sit on the grass outside the tent.

The touring was mostly across a wide plateau and it was here, some 3,000 feet up that Neterhat, the 'summer retreat' of the Governor of Bihar was situated. In fact 'The Chalet' there was rarely used and I often felt indignant about the money being spent by the Public Works Department on keeping up the house and the winding road leading up to it, ready for the Governor and his party, who in practice only went there for a few days in the hot weather, or not at all! Even yellow cosmos seeds had been scattered around by the gardeners which had spread over a wide area, providing a superb blaze of colour. Another favourite spot of ours was Rajadera where there was a large waterfall and pool in which we loved to swim. It was approached by a somewhat terrifying road with numerous bends. On one occasion when the brakes of our old Chevrolet car suddenly failed, our resourceful driver, Iltaf, negotiated the steep road downhill by tying the car with ropes to tree-trunks!

Another delightful part of the subdivision was Palkot where much of the land was owned by a wealthy *zemindar* (landlord), called the Baralal. He was married to a beautiful girl from the Nepal royal family. When we went there on tour I always visited her and I soon realised how difficult conversation was with a woman who had no interests apart from her clothes and children. When we first went there the Baralal had organised a bear-shoot for us and he was most disappointed when Bill admitted that he hated *shikar* and loathed killing animals purely for sport. So while the shoot went on, we left it, distressed to see a whole family of bears break out of cover and to then hear their cries as they were shot. The bears had white markings on their fur like V-necked sweaters!

Once while we were there Bill was approached by a group of villagers with a strange petition. It emerged that they were members of the Kharia tribe and belonged to a millenarian movement, the Thana Bhagats. The petition read like a European mediaeval document - the equivalent of 'When Adam delved and Eve span, who was then the gentleman?' It described the loss of their land to the Hindu landlords and the moneylenders and pleaded for the restitution of their old democratic rights which had existed when the world was young. This was one of the problems with which Bill became deeply involved during his years in Chota Nagpur.

Once a month we went to Ranchi, the district headquarters, for Bill to attend the monthly District Board meeting and discuss official matters with his Deputy Commissioner, Mr Merriman. At first we usually stayed with him and his wife who took us to the club in the evenings. It was here I had my first experience of a club and British social life in a small station. I hated it, for one was expected to play bridge, which I dreaded, and the conversation consisted of nothing but tittle-tattle about other members of the station. Bazaars run by the local ladies were frequently held where one was expected to purchase useless knick-knacks. How I agreed with the urbane Mr Merriman who told me that he wished a circular could be sent round to everyone by the club ladies saying that 'Unless you contribute X amount, you will be threatened with another bazaar.' I soon realised how empty and sad were the lives of most British women especially those whose children had been sent back to England to school and who had little to do. How different it was when later we stayed in Ranchi with Indian friends such as the family of the Forest Officer, Mr Subhawal. His house was always full of relatives with children sitting on the floor playing *chaupar* or *karam*, with grannies and aunties looking on knitting or busy with their household chores. We spent many happy weekends with this family which I shall always remember with delight.

From time to time we stayed with Mary Whitaker, an SPG missionary in Ranchi who was principal of the Guru Training School where Indian men were trained for teaching in the villages. Mary had a lively wit and read voraciously. She always had a stock of new books sent from England which she generously lent to us. There were also several of the young married ICS officers posted there such as the Walmsleys and the Brysons, whom I had known at Oxford, and whom I always enjoyed meeting again.

However, I found the quiet isolation of Gumla a great delight. It gave me a chance to read widely about India while Bill was in office. In those days it was possible to borrow reference books from the Imperial Library in Calcutta. They would be sent out by VPP (value payable post). I was able to borrow rare or expensive books such as the Reports of the Archaeological Survey of India, Bachofer's *Early Indian Sculpture*, Fergusson's *Tree and Serpent Worship*. In this way I was gradually able to get a basic knowledge of Indian art and history which was later to prove of the greatest value. I also began to mount and list the Kalighat and Maithil paintings which Bill had collected during his first years in India!

Life was never uneventful in Gumla. If anything interesting was happening in the office, Bill would send for me to hurry down and watch. I remember one occasion when Bill was trying a case in court and the Hindu complainant was taking an oath on the tail of a cow. It was a most comic sight - the cow refusing to stand still and evacuating copiously while the complainant solemnly endeavoured to hold its tail and take the oath. Sometimes when a dead man-eater tiger was brought in by its killer to claim the government reward, I would go down to the court to see the beautiful creature. But above all the quiet uneventful days at our headquarters enabled me to savour the sheer beauty of India's changing seasons and begin to read about its history.

* * *

In describing the Silver Jubilee at Gumla in 1935, Mildred Archer wrote to her parents in London on 8 May:

On Monday we had the final of the hockey knockout - the local High School v a local village. Then we presented the cups (at least I did) and after that distributed the enclosed photos to the crowd. Government sent down a heap of them. In the evening we had illuminations which were sweet - the effect is the same as electric bulbs, but what they do is to fix bamboos like this -

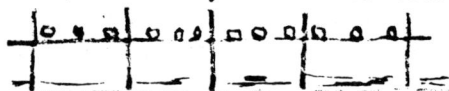

and then stand little earthern saucers (about 2" across) on them, (they cost Rs 1/- a thousand) and burn kerosene oil in them. As we shall sell the bamboos after the Jubilee is over, the illuminations won't cost much. People illuminate their houses like this during *Diwali*. The school children also attached paper flags to the bamboos, and the Public Works Department illuminated the court and erected an arch with Union Jacks and God Save the King on it! At 7.30 we had a firework display which was quite nice. The best item was a tree like this

which when lighted fell out like this -

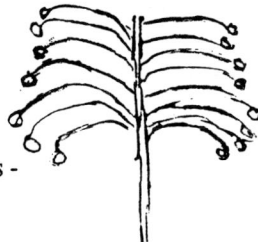

with red and blue sparks like flowers on the tips. After that the local villages came in to dance. They brought their flags with them, and erected them and danced round them. Every village has its flags - huge red and white ones this shape -

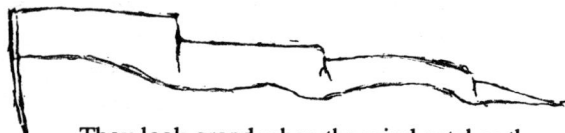

They look grand when the wind catches them.

Unfortunately only a few villages came as the Lutherans tried to sabotage it. Oh these missionaries do make me cross. Their two big campaigns are against 'Haria' drinking (rice beer) and this dancing. They hold that after the dancing there is a lot of immorality. Perhaps there is (although Mr. Lakra who is an aboriginal himself, says they exaggerate it terrifically). But I don't think the way to cure it is to abolish the dancing. It is the only art left to the aboriginals and it is the thing they enjoy most. If you saw the hordes of boys and girls turning up for it all laughing and singing you would love it. To abolish this would be to abolish one of the only bright spots in their lives. One of the missionaries came to Bill and asked if the women could be stopped from dancing as he thought it shameful for women to dance in public, but this sort of 'country dancing' seems to me far less sexey than European dancing. Don't you agree? The country dancing, is so vigorous and the boys and girls keep in separate lines, so that I can't see much harm in it. Similarly they attack the drinking. I agree that drunkeness is bad but the way to cure it, I think, is the way England has largely cured it, i.e. if the standard of living is raised and people have decent homes to stay

72

in, drunkeness declines just as Dad has always said about the change in London since you were children. These missionaries would endeavour to make people moral at the expense of all fun and cheerfulness. They would abolish dancing and put nothing in its place.

I would like them to have one small meal in two or three days in the hot weather and see if they didn't drink or dance in order to make life bearable. A lot of the missionaries arguments too have no relation to facts. Illegitimacy doesn't exist here. If the dancing led to continual claims for maintenance and deserted women with illegitimate children it would be different - but the villages are joint units and either the boy marries the girl after the child is born or else the child lives with the family. Each village keeps very much to itself and there are strong taboos about marriage outside the group. The result is that each group supports its members.

Unfortunately the dancing went on all night from 8 p.m. to 7 next morning and we got no sleep.

On Tuesday a local man gave a feast of rice and gur (rough unrefined sugar) to the poor - it consisted mainly of all the local urchins but as everyone is so thin and poor it didn't matter who turned up. Then there was a procession of school children with paper flags and they were given a feast of sweets afterwards. In the afternoon the Scouts gave a display - it was awful, Bill and I nearly died with laughing but we tried to look polite. Everything went wrong - their exercises were all out of time and some did arms downward bend when the mass did arms upward bend. Then they did a Zulu dance. Why should they do a Zulu dance when they have their own? Aren't scouts mad?

Worst of all was the singing as they tried to sing English scouts songs, but of course can't because their scales and everything are different in India. In the evening there was a magic lantern and lecturer sent by Government - coloured slides to show H.M.'s life. Bill had to stop it as the slides were so bad that no-one could see them. Bill and I couldn't tell if it was Queen Victoria or Alexander or Mary!

The lecturer was awful and said the same thing over and over again - 'H.M. saw the soldiers and was very happy, ('bahut kushi') 'H.M. saw Calcutta and was very happy, ('bahut kushi') H.M. went to Delhi and was very happy, ('bahut kushi'). People began to mimic him. That is where Government is up the pole. When we were in Ranchi we met Mr. Solomon, the government Publicity and Propaganda Secretary. He said the slides were bad but that the people were so simple and so easily pleased that they would love anything. This superior condescension makes me sick. These villagers have got their heads screwed on the right way and their remarks were worthy of cockneys. Half way through an old man said 'if Government is as good as you tell us why doesn't it send us better pictures?' And when an extra bad slide of Calcutta went up, one old chap said, 'Is this Queen Mary?' Bill and I rocked with laughter and eventually Bill made the man jump 20 slides and conclude. After that everyone shouted out 'Bus, Bus' (Enough, Enough) and rushed off to dance round their flags. There are also green little books about the life of the King in Hindi.

The pictures are so bad one can't tell who is who. I will send mine home when I have read it. Altogether the Jubilee was very funny and a good many people got a feed. I was amused by my little friends Sucri and Bisha. They were again in the van for everything. I saw them scrounging food for the poor and queuing up with the School boys (altho' they don't go to school) - they were everywhere in fact.

I do feel that the Jubilee is a racket though. It is interesting that this is the First Silver Jubilee to be celebrated - George IV, William IV and Victoria incidentally took no notice of theirs. It certainly seems that this is a timely bit of National Government propaganda, a gesture to the rest of Europe to show our political security.

Now the Jubilee is over and it is getting a bit warm in Gumla we have come up to our Summer residence of Rajadera. Dad will find it on the map up near Netterhat on the saddle-back. This is the coolest place in the subdivision. We left Gumla at 4.30 and drove along the saddle-back in the sunset and twilight. It was heavenly. We saw lots of peacocks which flew off squawking through the trees. You would love to see them - imagine an English wood with peacocks in it! We also saw lots of partridges and hares and some jungle murghis. These look so pretty - like farmyard cocks flying through the trees. Last night was ever so cool and we needed two blankets. I don't ever want to sleep indoors again - I woke up this morning at 5 to see the hills all round us black against the dawn - the sky all lemon and greeny blue and gold and then the sun came up over the hills and it was grand to feel it shine warm on one in bed. This is a heavenly place - you simply *must* come out one day.

Today Bill is doing rent suits, so I am spending the morning alone. The news Dad saw about communal trouble in Ranchi was very exaggerated. It was a trying business for the officers as there was so much persuasion and organisation necessary but it wasn't very serious so the troops used were a few Gurkhas who are always stationed in Ranchi and who supplemented the police.

17

Text Books

In November 1936 I spent a month staying in the SPG Mission at Ranchi, the headquarters town of Gumla subdivision. I was expecting our first child in December and as Gumla was some 86 miles from the hospital at Ranchi, along a rough and bumpy road, the Civil Surgeon advised that I should go to Ranchi a few weeks beforehand and stay there so as to be near the hospital. I spent that month with Mary Whitaker. I had already come to know some of the other SPG missionaries, especially Marjorie Hughes, the headmistress of St Margaret's High School for Girls (another SPG institution in Ranchi). She had sometimes come out to Gumla and stayed with us when she was inspecting schools in the subdivision. With a month ahead of me, I thought it would be more interesting and comfortable to stay quietly at the Mission rather than with ICS colleagues where I would get caught up in the social round at the club.

Soon after my arrival, several Indian teachers at the school happened to fall ill and I was asked if I could possibly help by taking the Matriculation Class for English! On looking at the text books I was told to use, I was amazed at their lack of relationship to the vocabulary or experience of aboriginal or Bihari girls who had never been outside the town or its immediate environs. The text-books used by the school and published by the OUP, MacMillan or Longman's Green were good but clearly intended for English children. They seemed utterly unsuitable for the Indian girls at St Margaret's. I remember that the first lesson I had to give was linked to a poem by Robert Louis Stevenson in *The Child's Garden of Verses* which was a set book. It included the lines:

'And I can hear the thrushes singing
In the lilacs on the lawn.'

How to communicate the meaning of these words or convey their associations to Indian children?

I returned to Mary Whitaker's bungalow that day full of youthful indignation, and found that she whole-heartedly agreed with me about the inappropriate choice of text books by the Bihar Text Book Committee but admitted that the choice was very limited. Later she suggested that we should co-operate and write a series of text books ourselves - I should write a text and she, with her long experience of teaching in India, would see that what I wrote was appropriate for each age-group and she would write the accompanying exercises. We would endeavour to use only material that related to India and came within the children's own experience. We included local folk tales and only referred to birds or animals with which the children were familiar.

It was while staying in Ranchi that I began to consider recruiting an ayah to help me. I heard that a tribal girl, Mariam, who had been an infant-teacher at the mission school, had had an illegitimate child by one of the High School boys. Because the boy was of a different caste, his parents would not allow the couple to marry, and the boy had been sent away to work in Calcutta. On hearing that I needed an ayah the Mission suggested that Mariam might come and work for us. The arrangement proved a great success. She stayed with us until we had to leave India in 1947 and her child, Sushil, proved a delightful playmate for our own children. I still hear from him regularly every Christmas. When we left India in 1947 we arranged a marriage for Mariam. Everything seemed satisfactory but sadly, a year later she died in childbirth.

18

Purnea

Meanwhile in March 1937 Bill had been transferred from Gumla to Purnea in North Bihar as District Magistrate, in charge now, not of a subdivision, but of a District consisting of three subdivisions - Kishanganj, Araria and Purnea Sadr. The contrast to Gumla was in every way dramatic, and I quickly realised how impossible it is to generalise about 'India' or a 'province'. In place of the jungly hills, small villages and the tribal population of Ranchi district, the sprawling town of Purnea was situated on a flat bare grassy plain with a population of Hindus and Muslims. Purnea lay to the extreme north-east of Bihar province. To the north, the district adjoined Nepal and the dense forests of the Terai, the foothills of the Himalayas. To the south was the great Ganges River and to the west the Kosi, another huge river descending from the Himalayas, which over the centuries had constantly changed its course and had swung from side to side flooding the land and leaving behind a great wilderness of sand that could not be cultivated, but became the haunt of tiger, leopards and rhinoceros (the latter now sadly extinct). To the east the alluvial plain stretched into Bengal. There were so many flat and uncultivated areas in parts of the district that in the cold weather one could drive the car across open stretches of grassy plain with no sign of a road.

In place of our tiny house at Gumla, we now had a large white classical bungalow of the early 19th century type with wide pillared verandahs front and back and a large porte-cochère. The rooms were spacious with green-shuttered French windows opening on to the verandahs. The house stood in a vast park-like compound. A small oval plot in front had at some time been intended for a flower-garden and had been fenced in to keep out animals. Within it was a solitary mauve-blossomed bauhinea tree and traces of neglected brick-edged flower beds. To the left was a large, shady tamarind tree, alive with birds, under which the *chaprassis* and visitors waiting to see Bill would squat. At the back the compound was bounded by a distant railway line along which once a day in the early evening a small train solemnly puffed.

This 'chuff-chuff' was a great attraction for our small son who would rush out to see it. In the evenings, especially during the Rains when the dust had settled, a ghostly line of snowy peaks - the Himalayas - appeared shining pink in the sunset. As dusk fell flying-foxes would wing their way across the sky and come to feed on the fruit of a large banyan tree in the garden. We delighted in watching them as they settled for the night chattering to each other and hanging upside down on the branches like dark pods.

The Europeans in Purnea, like the landscape, were a complete contrast to those in Ranchi district. We had entered the world of Kipling and the indigo-planting days. Our nearest neighbours were all retired planters living in run-down bungalows situated like our house in huge undemarcated grassy compounds. Until the First World War and especially in the 1890s Purnea had been a flourishing and wealthy indigo-growing district but competition from German aniline dyes had killed the industry. Sugar-cane and jute had now taken over. We frequently came across great deserted indigo vats as we toured the district. Most of the old planters had now sold up and retired to England before the War, but a few, most of whom had some Indian blood in their veins, had stayed on. Apart from their houses and compounds they possessed little. A few faithful servants had stayed with them. The large bungalows, once shining white, were now neglected and green with damp-stains. The dark shuttered rooms were furnished with heavy old-fashioned teak furniture, with faded photographs on the walls and moth-eaten hunting trophies around. When one approached these bungalows it was as though they were deserted with no sign of life. The first time I went to visit one, I saw a solitary figure scuttle inside but when I called no answer came. Life in Purnea seemed suspended.

But gradually I came to know the owners and encouraged them to talk. Most of the women were unmarried or widowed and there were almost no children. They never talked about the present, only the past. Apart from their servants, the only link they seemed to have with Indians was the local Raja, PC Lall, and his family. They looked forward to the occasional celebrations provided by him, such as the weddings of his sons, to which he would invite them all. The Raja was a cheerful individual, chiefly interested in racing in Calcutta and Darjeeling. He had a handsome, large, matronly wife, who, it was said, had saved the life of the Governor of Bengal, Sir John Anderson, at the Darjeeling Races in 1934 by interposing herself between him and a would-be assassin. They constantly recalled the time when their families were rich and powerful during the great indigo days. The men spoke of fishing and *shikar* expeditions, showed off their trophies and recalled the names of famous *shikaris* such as Shillingford, who had killed numerous tigers and rhinoceros, for Purnea had been renowned for its abundant game, now almost extinct. I sometimes visited two lady-like old sisters, then in their 70s - the Misses Cave (jokingly referred to by everyone as the 'Cave Women'). They wore long shapeless dresses reaching almost to the ground, and every day at 4 o'clock they presided over a little tea-table on the verandah set with a silver teapot and silver muffin-dishes containing tiny triangular sandwiches, the whole table shrouded with embroidered organdie covers weighted with bead tassels at the corners to keep off the flies. They would sadly talk of the 'old days' with their great tennis and croquet parties, races and visits from the Governor.

Our nearest neighbour was of a very different type. Dicky Downing, the District Engineer lived with his old mother, his wife, Ruby, and their young daughter in a modern Public Works Department bungalow adjacent to our house. He too came of planter stock and was descended from a branch of the famous Palmer family, the great Calcutta Agency firm and bankers, members of which had retired to Purnea in the early 19th century. Earlier still in the 18th century, a forebear, General William Palmer of the Bengal Army, had had two Muslim wives. (Many years later in the 1950s I was able to identify a delightful oil painting of this family by Francesco Renaldi which was hanging in the old India Office in Whitehall). The Purnea Palmers had built 'Palmer's Bundh', a great embankment which kept the flood-waters away from Purnea Town. In the cool of the evening I would frequently wheel Michael in his pram round to the Downings' bungalow and listen to old Mrs Downing's stories of the past. She had had 20 children, but at the age of almost 80 was still spry and played a gentle game of badminton with me. She recalled how in the old days at the onset of the hot weather, all the planters' children would go up to school in Darjeeling in a great cavalcade on horseback accompanied only by their servants. She and her husband would go down to Calcutta once a year by riverboat to stock up with stores and clothing, buying literally dozens of boots and shoes to last her huge family for the whole year. She had some fine furniture and possessions and many years later in 1970 when my husband was Keeper of the Indian Department of the Victoria and Albert Museum, he acquired a *pan* box and bidri-ware *attardan* or scent sprinkler from Dicky Downing for the Museum which Dicky said had formerly belonged to his ancestor William Palmer. Dicky had a deep knowledge of the district and he showed me many decaying monuments,

Faiz Baksh, the wife of William Palmer, with two of their children, Mary and Hastings (detail from the picture painted by Renaldi, c.1786)

including a lonely cenotaph deep in the grass on the edge of our own compound which marked the grave of a planter who had lived with a Muslim lady in the huge bungalow nearby. Dicky also had many *shikar* stories. I remember one, of how a friend of his had shot a python and loaded it into the car so that he could take it home and skin it to make shoes for his wife. On his way back, he looked into the mirror of the car and saw the python jauntily rising up on the seat immediately behind him!

The Station Club was frequented chiefly by these old planters with the addition of a few retired Government servants. One of these, jocularly known as 'The Admiral', had been a pilot on the Hooghly River. From him I heard many stories about the shifting sand-banks, the sinking sands, the tigers and other problems of negotiating this dangerous river (information which later, when I was working at the India Office Library, brought to life the early engravings of the river that were in my charge and highlighted the dangers for the great East Indiamen as they made their way up the river to Calcutta). There was no ban on Indians going to the Station Club - a few from time to time did go to play bridge or billiards - but I soon realised the tragedy of the old Anglo-Indians who stood isolated between two worlds - looked down upon both by most Indians and by British officials who made caustic comments about 'a touch of the tar-brush', 'chee-chee accents' and 'slim ankles'. The Station Club was, I felt, a sad and depressing place.

Far more cheerful was the Town Club with its new building and tennis courts. Here the Indian provincial service officers, clerks and pleaders would go to play tennis or cards and it was here that Bill and I usually went for tennis in the evenings. There could be no greater contrast than that between the laughter and leg-pulling at the Town Club and the sad depressing atmosphere with its talk of 'the good old days' at the Station Club.

A number of experiences in Purnea were to have strange links with my career in England some 30 years later. On a visit in 1936 to Mr. Merriman, who was then our Commissioner in Bhagalpur (the district headquarters) I was taken by him for an evening stroll along the bank of the Ganges beside which his bungalow was situated. On this walk he showed me a monument to Augustus Cleveland, a former East India Company servant, which had been erected to commemorate his death in 1784 aged 29. The inscription noted how he 'after employing only the means of conciliation, confidence and benevolence, attempted and accomplished the entire subjection of the lawless and savage inhabitants of the Jungle-Terry of Rajemehal'. Merriman told me how Cleveland had become attracted to the Paharias, the tribal people in his district, who at that time were regarded as 'savages' as they frequently attacked travellers moving through the district. Cleveland gained their trust and organised a number of them into a Corps of 'Hill Rangers' who themselves policed the whole area. I little realised that a few years later these same people would be in Bill's own district. Nearby on a hillock overlooking the Ganges was Cleveland's house, a large old classical mansion, at that time occupied as a summer retreat by a branch of the Tagore family and today I understand, owned by Calcutta University. Many years later, when working on the careers of the British artists William Hodges and Thomas Daniell, I encountered Cleveland and his house again. He became a generous patron of Hodges, and took him out on tour in the district in 1780. Hodges made a drawing of a Paharia village which he later published as an engraving in his *Select Views in India* (1785-8). A copy of this was made by Lady Jones, when her husband, the great Sanskrit scholar Sir William, was staying with Cleveland in Bhagalpur. This drawing I later found in the collection of the Royal Asiatic Society in London. Nor did I know that Bill and I would later, when back in England, purchase an oil-painting by Thomas Daniell of Cleveland's house, opposite which I am now sitting as I write. It was painted by Thomas when he and his nephew, William, were staying there with Samuel Davis, a successor of Cleveland, and were working up their watercolours into oils for sale at a lottery of their paintings to be held in Calcutta in 1790. The painting shows the fine Palladian house on the hill beside the river on which an elephant-headed pleasure-boat is sailing. It was along that very bank that I had walked with the Commissioner in the evenings.

It was also during that visit that I first became aware of the scholarly contribution to the study of Indian history and culture that had been made by so many of the British members of the Indian Civil Service and the Indian Army. The day after my walk along the river bank, I spent the morning alone in the Merrimans' house. He and Bill were attending a District Board Meeting and Mrs Merriman was out playing morning-bridge, from which I had excused myself. Alone in the sitting room, I browsed among Mr Merriman's books. A large tome attracted me, entitled *Annals of Rajasthan* by James Tod. I had never heard of it and it at once opened up a new world. On the shelf below was a long run of volumes, *Bengal Past and Present*, the journal of the Calcutta Historical Society. This too came as a delightful surprise, with its detailed recording of recondite information about the province and Calcutta, contributed mainly by members of the ICS and the Indian Army. Mr Merriman returned before his wife and talked enthusiastically to me about

Cleveland House at Bhagalpur, by Thomas Daniell, 1790 (detail on front cover)

Bhagalpur and its history. I suddenly realised how British social life in India forced many scholarly people to hide their knowledge and true interests behind a conventional facade. When I first arrived in Bihar in 1934, I had met John Merriman at the Club in Ranchi and had regarded him as an urbane, hard-drinking social charmer. For a short time that morning before the return of the others, he revealed his scholarly interests and his wide knowledge of the province and its history which I found fascinating. My few days in his company later helped me identify work by Hodges and the Daniells when cataloguing the drawings in the India Office Library made by British artists in India in the 18th and early 19th centuries as they travelled up and down the Ganges. He had introduced me to a world with which I later became deeply involved.

MA with young Michael and her brother, Frank Bell, at Ghum, 1937

It was from Purnea too that I made my first acquaintance with the Himalayas. I went to Darjeeling for a few weeks in the hot weather of 1938 as Michael had grown pale and wan and plagued with prickly-heat. I stayed at a boarding house run by a Mrs Weatherall who was descended from one of the old Purnea families. I believe the first generation had come out to serve in the Police in the mid 19th century and one of them figures in the novel *Indigo*. The change in Michael was dramatic - in a few days he was well and lively again. I shall never forget waking up my first morning in Darjeeling and looking out of the window. The icy peak of Kanchenjunga was shining pink in the rising sun and I had to crick my neck to see the summit. It seemed almost on top of me. I remembered Edward Lear's ambivalent reactions when trying to paint it: 'Kanchenjunga', he wrote 'is not, so it seems to me, a sympathetic mountain - it is so very Godlike and stupendous and all that great world of dark open valley full of misty, hardly to be imagined forms.' I found it breath-takingly beautiful. I was not in Darjeeling long enough to explore the surrounding area with its great forests plunging down to rushing streams. The hill-people, especially the women in their beautiful Tibetan-style costume, were most attractive. They were also incredibly strong. I was amazed at seeing an old lady climbing up a steep hill carrying an upright piano on her back supported only by a leather head-band! Bill joined us for a few days and we moved on to a strange boarding house at Ghum just outside Darjeeling where the crazy landlady lost her temper with her servants one evening and threw the crockery down the *khud*! We could not visit Nepal during our time in Purnea, although it was so near, for in 1937 it was still 'closed' to the British, although there were British 'political' links with the state. One of Bill's tiresome duties as Collector of Purnea was to don morning-dress and a white topi and stand on the Purnea railway station platform whenever the Maharaja passed through by train on his way to Calcutta, 'in case there was anything he needed'. This event usually took place soon after dawn when the Maharaja was fast asleep in his saloon coach and was never in need of any help or attention!

In February 1939 Bill and I, with Michael left Purnea and went on leave to England via Ranchi. Home leave to England occurred only every four or five years unless there were special reasons such as serious ill health.

19

The Voyage in War Time

As we set out rumours of war were already gathering. Towards the end of August 1939, Bill was suddenly recalled to India, along with all the other Indian Civil Servants who were on leave in England. He was ordered to report at Glasgow and wait there for a passage. On 3 September, the very day that war was declared, they sailed. I was left behind with Michael aged two and a half years. My father immediately hastened to the High Commission in Aldwych and managed to fix a return passage for us. We sailed from Tilbury in mid-September. I had no idea of where Bill was going to be posted on his return and where he would be when I arrived, for all letters were being censored.

It was a strange voyage. The passengers consisted almost entirely of women and children with only a few men - chiefly munition-workers and engineers who were being drafted to factories in India, such as that at Cossipore. We sailed in a huge convoy of boats of many different types. The wire netting had been taken down from the sides of the deck to ease evacuation in case of an emergency. A small child like Michael could easily have squeezed through the rails, so I immediately attached reins to him and tethered him up whenever I had to leave him even for five minutes. As soon as we entered the English Channel, destroyers began circling around us all the time on the look-out for submarines. On the second day I was bathing Michael before putting him to bed, when suddenly the whole boat juddered in the most terrifying way. I quickly wrapped him in a towel and hurried up on deck. One of the destroyers accompanying us had dropped a depth charge, but it appeared to be a false alarm so we returned to our cabins. We were fortunate not to be attacked throughout the voyage but conditions were very different from the peace-time voyage of 1934, when I first went to India. There was no going on shore, no sightseeing at the ports, no organised amusements and the ship was 'blacked out' every evening. The passengers without children were put on look-out duty during the day to report any unusual object they could see in the water in case it was a periscope or a floating mine.

Although we went through the Suez Canal, the return voyage took about three months, for we proceeded at the rate of the slowest cargo boat in the convoy. Until we reached the Suez Canal, the ships were all spread out with the destroyers rushing around the whole group like sheepdogs. At night the formation changed and the ships went into single-file. One morning I went up on to the deck soon after dawn and watched the change of formation take place. The commanding ship ran up its signals and gradually all the boats, which were in a long line like a caterpillar stretching far into the distance, came closer together and merged into a great huddled group. The slow manoeuvre was a most impressive sight.

Censorship had already begun so I had no way of informing Bill that I was on my way back to India. It was not until Michael and I reached Madras in December that I was able to go on shore and send a telegram to the Bihar Government asking them to inform Bill that I was returning. Fortunately this was efficiently done and on reaching Calcutta, Bill and our driver, Iltaf, were waiting on the quayside for us. How lucky we were to be reunited, for after 1940, with the sinking of ships, all passages were cancelled and like many other families we would have been separated for the duration of the war.

20

The Census, Hazaribagh

Bill told me that he had been posted as Provincial Census Superintendent to Hazaribagh, a small country town in Bihar to the north of Ranchi. This had been chosen for the 1942 Census Headquarters as it was centrally placed for touring over the whole province. The town lay on the 'New Military Road' which had been constructed in 1782 for troops and travellers going from Calcutta to Benares. Years later I was able to acquire for the India Office Library a sketch-book by Sir Charles D'Oyly depicting this very road and neighbourhood in 1825 soon after it had been built.

Hazaribagh fortunately had little conventional social life, but there were many kind and pleasant people living there, mostly Anglo-Indians. We had an old-fashioned bungalow facing the *maidan* where the Cadets from the Police Training College exercised their horses every morning. Like Ranchi, the town was surrounded by picturesque hills and forests. To the south was Parasnath Hill, some 4,480 feet high, named after the Jain Tirthankara, or saint Parsvanath, who was said to have attained Nirvana by fasting to death on the mountain. There were rocky hills all over the district and Bill often spent the evenings rock-climbing. He taught our driver, Iltaf, how to climb with ropes and Michael was also introduced to this sport and taken on the easier climbs.

'Census Superintendent' was a post Bill had always coveted as he knew it would give him a chance to tour the whole province, gain an overall view of its people and a knowledge of the great variety of castes and cultures that existed in Bihar. Over the years there had grown up a fine tradition of scholarly Census Reports by ICS officers. In Bihar, for example, there had been Sir Edward Gait's report of 1922 and Graham Lacey's Report of 1932. Bill was clearly an obvious choice for this post as he had already published ethnographic material. It was here that we first met Verrier Elwin who was to become one of our greatest friends.

In 1935 the old anthropologist, Surat Chanda Roy, the editor of *Man in India,* whom we had earlier met in Ranchi, had just died and Bill and

Verrier Elwin were invited by his family to undertake the joint editorship of the journal, a job which they continued until 1946. This was the beginning of an exhilarating partnership. Bill was already a great admirer of Elwin's work and now they had a chance to meet and work together, a collaboration which enriched the writings of both of them and led to their joint editorship of the periodical. We had long known Verrier by reputation, admired his writings and been attracted by his unconventional approach to life. Verrier had done brilliantly at Oxford. He was a don at Merton, took Holy Orders and then went to India to work for the Christa Seva Sangh (an Anglican High Church Missionary Society). After a spell in Bombay he joined Mahatma Gandhi at his *ashram*. He often related amusing stories to us about the 'hot-house' atmosphere among Gandhi's lady followers. He then worked among the tribal people of Central India but instead of converting them, he was 'converted' by them and he shed his Holy Orders and gradually moved into the field of anthropology. We always looked forward to his unconventional visits. There is no doubt that he enjoyed shocking officialdom. When he came to stay with us later at Patna, he 'called' at Government House to sign 'the book', dressed in sandals, bright blue trousers and a lurid shirt. The ADC on duty was clearly uneasy at the apparition!

The fact that the Census recurred every ten years meant that its general organisation existed in the Secretariat 'on paper' and could be quickly swung into action. The census in India involved far more than mere enumeration. The organisation had to be set up all over the province long before the actual counting took place. Enumerators had to be appointed and trained about the questions that had to be put to the villagers - questions about caste, religion, language and occupation. Every hut and house in the province had to be given a number so that all its occupants could be accurately recorded when the final day came. Bill had to tour continually over the whole province checking that the organisation was ready and that the enumerators knew and understood their duties. In this way he gained a wonderful knowledge of the whole area. In the course of his visits he was able to make time for amassing further information for himself on subjects that excited him. In Shahabad, where he had begun his official life, he was able to collect further information about the Birnath cult which he was later to use in his book, *The Vertical Man*, published in 1947. He also made a large collection of Bhojpuri Marriage Songs. These were published in the vernacular in the *Bihar and Orissa Research Journal* of 1942 and 1943. He planned to publish a description of the marriage ritual and its symbolism, but it was still unfinished when he died.

However, with the help of Professor Stoller Miller of Columbia University I have been able to publish much of this material in *Songs for the Bride* (1985). During his tours Bill was able to return to Mithila to do further work on Maithila Painting and make a further collection of Maithil paintings. In this way much folk culture which might have perished has been recorded, and is now in the India Office Library.

Bill was greatly disappointed when, as a war-economy, it was decided not to publish a full Census Report but only the population statistics. However, much of this material has eventually been published through other channels. The Census brought Bill into touch with other scholars working on similar ethnographic material. Among these was George Grigson, elder brother of the poet, Geoffrey Grigson, who was working on the tribes in the Central Provinces. It also led to his meeting Christoph von Furer Haimendorf. In 1939 when war broke out, Christoph had been researching on the Nagas of Assam, and was about to return to Austria. In view of his nationality he was at once interned. With great foresight, Sir Theodore Tasker in Hyderabad was able to get him released so that he could continue to work on the tribal people of Andhra Pradesh on condition that he reported his whereabouts regularly to Government and the Police. It was through Christoph that we later came to know Philip Mills and later Professor Hutton, both of whom had been Deputy Commissioners in the Naga Hills and had written about its people and their culture.

I myself found this period extremely stimulating. I was forced to live a somewhat circumscribed life at that time. Michael was still a small boy and in 1940 our daughter Margaret was born. I was ill with thrombosis after her birth and could not tour widely as I had before, especially as Bill was moving over the whole province and it would have been impossible to accompany him with a new-born baby. However I was able to meet these various scholars and help with the editing of *Man in India* from Hazaribagh.

During this period Chandra Shekar Jha, whom I had known while I was at Oxford, had come to Hazaribagh as Deputy Commissioner. By now he had married a beautiful young Maithil Brahmin girl, Lakshmi. Chandra had a distinguished career in the ICS and was later to become Ambassador to France and Turkey after Independence and then Indian Representative at the United Nations. I like to think that I helped Lakshmi a little during her years in Hazaribagh when she had recently come out of *purdah* and was very unsure of herself and shy. I, for my part, learnt much from her about orthodox Brahmin life. We kept in touch after Independence and it is a great delight that when my daughter and grandson visited India they were able to meet the Jhas in Delhi where they had retired. Sadly Lakshmi died soon after but I was able to meet her husband Chandra again on returning to Delhi in 1989 before he too died later that year.

mural

21

Patna

When in 1940 Bill heard a rumour that with the ending of the Census he was to be posted to Patna, his heart sank. It brought back unhappy memories of his arrival in India in 1931 and the stiff social life which had confirmed his worst fears about the kind of British India he was about to encounter. Nor had his first glance at the New City attracted him. It seemed a symbol of British aloofness and reminded him of his first lonely days in India. It reminded him too, of EM Forster's description of Patna in *A Passage to India*. 'Edged rather than washed by the River Ganges, it trails for a couple of miles along the bank, scarcely distinguishable from the rubbish it deposits so freely. There is no painting and scarcely any carving in the bazaars. The very wood seems to be made of mud, the inhabitants of mud moving. As for the civil station itself, it provokes no emotion, it charms not, neither does it repel, it is sensibly planned, it has nothing hideous in it and only the view is beautiful. It shares nothing with the city except the overarching sky.' At the same time in 1940 we had heard another rumour that Bill was to be posted to Monghyr, a city on the Ganges to the east of Patna where there was an old Fort. This had been welcome news, but the Secretariat had discovered that Ahmad, an Indian ICS officer, who had been selected to go to Patna as Collector, owned property there. No officer was ever allowed to go to a district where he owned property or had financial interests of any kind, so the Secretariat switched the two postings round and sent Ahmad to Monghyr and Bill to Patna.

On arriving we were given a newly-built two-storied house on the edge of the *maidan* at Bankipore which lay halfway between the Old and the New Cities. Here we had electricity, sanitation and a telephone for the first time. Bill's predecessor had lived in a fine old bungalow on the bank of the Ganges, but this had been condemned by the health authorities as kites had an unpleasant habit of dropping into the garden pieces of human flesh which they had scavenged from the corpses at the nearby burning ghats! A new house had therefore been built for the Collector. It was close to the Gola Ghar, a strange beehive-shaped granary which had been built in 1786 under orders from Warren Hastings as a precaution against famine. In our time this was being used as a store for office furniture, but during the famine of 1942 it was again used for its original purpose. Michael loved to climb up the stone stairs which encircled the outside, to sit on the top looking out across the great expanse of the Ganges, up which the slow-moving sailing boats passed to and fro. There was a tradition that the Nepal ruler Shamsher Jang had once ridden a horse up those same steps.

Contrary to our fears, this posting was to prove a most significant part of our lives, introducing us to sophisticated Indian art and resulting in several deep and lasting friendships with Indian collectors. We first met there the famous scholar and art historian, Rai Krishna Dasa of Benares, when he came to Patna in 1941 to deliver the Ram Din lectures on 'Indian Painting'. He became a great friend and we were to spend several return visits to India after Independence staying with him at Benares where we always met a large group of his friends from the nearby University who would gather every evening at his house to discuss Indian painting and sculpture. It was also in Patna that we first met Gopi Krishna Kanoria, who owned one of the greatest collections of Indian miniatures. He introduced us to Sanskrit and Hindi poetry which he would recite and then translate while he was showing us the paintings. Gopi, who later came regularly to England after Independence for medical treatment, always stayed with us and became my husband's greatest Indian friend. We kept his special cooking vessels in a separate cupboard in our kitchen in London so that his 'orthodox' wife could always accompany him to England and cook for him. On return visits to India we stayed many times with him at Patna or in his 'country' house in Benares on the bank of the Ganges. It had a pleasant garden sloping down to the river with a little temple on the bank. I can remember Bill once becoming impatient at the noise of the resident priest who was constantly ringing his bell and chanting. Bahuji (Gopi's wife) at once called on him to desist. He replied that he was only doing 'God's work' 'Bhagwan ka kam.' Bahuji answered sharply 'Bhagwan ka kam jaldi khatam karo!' (Finish off God's work quickly.) Gopi kept his paintings in his house wrapped in great bundles of red insect-proof cloth. We would spend the evenings leafing through the miniatures, while Gopi commented on each one, often chanting verses linked to the subject-matter and identifying the style and subject.

Another great attraction of Patna was the Museum of which Bill was ex-officio chairman. It possessed one of the greatest pieces of Indian sculpture - the 'Didarganj Yakshi', of the 1st century BC. This was a great female standing figure holding a fly-whisk over her shoulder. The Museum also possessed a huge collection of little terracotta figurines c.2000 BC, which were frequently washed out of the river-banks in the Rains. I still have two such terracottas standing on the mantelpiece of the room in which I am writing now. There was also a great library in Patna, the Khuda Baksh, which had a fine collection of illustrated Arabic and Persian manuscripts.

While in Patna, I was asked to serve on the Text-Book Committee which had prescribed my 'Bihar Readers' for use in Bihar schools. I was also approached by Moinul Huq, the Principal of the BN College, to edit and write an introduction to William Morris's *Atalanta's Race*, which was to be a set-book for the Bachelor of Arts English course, in Bihar. The poem seemed to me to be a very strange choice for Indian students, but I endeavoured to give it some relevance by discussing Morris's role in trying to save handicrafts and preserve the artistic values of pre-industrial societies, work which enthusiasts such as Pupul Jayakar are continuing in India today. I was also put on the Text-Book Committee. This was an interesting experience for me, as in my innocence, I had been unaware of the financial pressure that publishers' representatives try to put on members of such committees who prescribe books for use in schools and universities. Fortunately I was never approached or faced with these problems directly, but I learnt much about these practices from other members of the Committee.

During our time in Patna we made a number of good friends, among them Fazlur Rahman, a brilliant young professor of English at Patna University. He and Bill would sit up until late at night discussing modern English poetry. We also came to know a number of the leading Congress politicians such as Rajendra Prasad (later the First President of India), and Dr Mahmud, who had been a friend of EM Forster during his time in India. Forster had stayed with him and Ross Masood for about eight months when he revisited Patna. He had already part-finished *A Passage to India*. He had then got stuck and put it by for some years and only after coming back again to Patna was he able to finish it off. Bill asked Mahmud about the trial scene in this book where one of the British was sitting on the dais beside the Indian magistrate. We had always thought this utterly improbable although symbolically true for the novel. Mahmud agreed that it could not have happened in recent years, but he himself remembered how earlier, before 1921, there was indeed 'Planter's Raj' in Tirhut district in North Bihar, and in places like Chapra and Muzaffarpur, where the planters endeavoured to put moral pressure on magistrates in cases involving other Europeans by attending court in a group and being given seats near the magistrate. Forster, whom we later met in London, admitted that he owed much to Dr Mahmud while planning his novel and that Mahmud had told him much about life in Bihar in 'the old days' which undoubtedly did influence him.

But above all, the posting to Patna led to our meeting PC Manuk, the leading barrister in Patna and the owner of one of the finest collections of Indian miniatures. We also met other collectors such as Jalan, an 'orthodox' businessman in Patna city who also had a collection. Our friendships led to the development of our own interests in Indian miniature painting. We started to study the subject and to acquire miniatures ourselves from the dealers who came to Patna to visit Manuk and Jalan. Bill had first met Manuk through his court work and through the Patna Museum where they were both on the managing committee. When Manuk died he left his great collection to be divided between the Victoria and Albert Museum, the British Museum and the FitzWilliam Museum in Cambridge where he had been an undergraduate.

Manuk employed an old man, Ishwari Prasad (born c.1870) and his son to mount and do minor repairs to his miniatures. Ishwari was descended from Fakir Chand Lal (c.1770 - c.1865), a painter who had come to Patna from Murshidabad. I came to know him well. In his spotless white *dhoti* and little round black hat, he would come to our bungalow and reminisce to me about his forebears. He also related his family's memories of Sir Charles D'Oyly, Company servant (1781-1845) who was Opium Agent at Patna from 1821 to 1831. D'Oyly himself was a talented amateur artist who encouraged the local painters to work for him. When Bill retired from the ICS in 1947 we purchased Ishwari's private collection, all of which is now in the India Office Library and the Victoria and Albert Museum.

22

To the Hills

In the hot weathers of 1942-45 I regularly took Michael and Margaret up to Mussoorie for a spell of about four months. Until then I had always sworn that I would not leave my husband and go to the Hills, nor would I if I had been alone. But when in the hot weather the children became ill with tummy troubles, and developed mango boils and prickly heat which easily became septic, I succumbed like many other mothers before me and retreated to the Hills.

The journey was always welcomed by the children. For a whole day and two nights the express train sped from Patna to Dehra Dun across the great northern plain. We always booked a first class compartment with a lavatory, wash basin and four bunks, two on each side one above the other, which were converted at night into four beds. Our bearer accompanied us in the servants compartment and our ayah, Mariam, and her little boy, Sushil, shared the compartment with us. From time to time when the train stopped the bearer looked in to see if we were comfortable and at night he came in to spread the bedding rolls.

The journey always brought home to me the vast size of India and its immense population - great crowds patiently waiting at every station along the line and the endless fawn plain, a mixture of monotony and magic, that stretched mile after mile from Bihar to the foothills of the Himalayas. At night the darkness and monotonous clunkety clunk of the train was punctuated at the stations by a sudden blaze of light, the clamour of passengers and the harsh cry of '*pan, biri, cigarettes*'. Each morning revealed the beautiful dawn light and the same brown plain dotted with villages, great mango trees and palms, the villagers setting out for their fields with their herds of cattle in a cloud of dust.

At the first stop after dawn, a crowd would quickly alight from the train to ease themselves beside the railway line, clean their teeth and break their fast, while tea-sellers, carrying their wares on their heads, hurried up and down the platform crying '*garam cha, cha garam*'. We always took food and drink with us to last the whole journey but the railway supplied a great zinc tub containing a block of ice which was set on the floor of the compartment between the berths with the electric fan directed on to it. As the ice gently melted, it cooled the compartment. One night when the train stopped with a sudden jerk, I woke to find that Michael had rolled off his bunk and was still fast asleep on top of the slopping slab of ice!

Certain places on the journey were always welcomed by the children every year. There was the huge bridge where the railway line crosses the Son River, a tributary of the Ganges. They would cranc out of the windows to look down through the great girders at the river below. Benares station too was a delight as it teemed with monkeys. One year when the train stopped there a great creature leapt into the compartment through the open window and carried off the bunch of bananas which I had just set out for our meal. The children watched with fascination as it sat on a railway wagon opposite our carriage, delicately peeling the fruit and impudently devouring it in front of us.

At last Dehra Dun was reached early on the second morning and we disembarked. A taxi took us to Mussoorie zigzaging crazily up the hill. Immediately we began to feel a delightful chill in the air and soon jerseys and cardigans had to be put on. At Rajkot where the road suddenly narrowed, we transferred to rickshaws for the last part of the journey to 'The Deodars'.

This old-fashioned boarding house at Mussoorie stood on a spur of the hills above the so-called 'Happy Valley', facing out across to distant Chakrata and the great mountains to the north. On clear days a line of snows could be seen stretching from end to end of the horizon. In the middle distance was a great grassy hill, Ben Og, rising above the forest. Each year I rented a tiny two-roomed cottage in a large garden poised among deodar trees looking down on to the steep valley below, where great lammergeiers constantly wheeled or plunged and langur monkeys swung chattering through the trees. Long days stretched ahead of me but I was always busy looking after the children, teaching them or reading, and in 1942 marking English BA and MA papers for Patna University which were sent up to me by post.

'The Deodars' belonged to a cultivated old Anglo-Indian lady, Miss Swetenham, and was run as a private boarding house. The same families came to stay with her every year, mainly missionaries, teachers and doctors. I found a good friend there in Dr Harvey, a young medical missionary from Ludhiana, with her little girl and German governess, Trudi. There was also Dr Philpot, a Professor of Mathematics at Benares University, who with his wife was another regular visitor. I had time to read voraciously. At first I ordered parcels of books, mainly Indian history and 19th century memoirs, which were sent up to me in parcels from the Imperial Library, Calcutta, but I soon discovered that Miss Swetenham herself had an excellent library. It was from her that I borrowed a first edition of Fanny Parks's delightful *Wanderings of a Pilgrim in search of the Picturesque* (1850) and learnt that a house called 'Cloud End', the building of which Fanny Parks was supervising in 1838 for her relative 'Captain S.', belonged to Miss Swetenham herself and that the 'Captain S.' of the journal was Captain F Swetenham, an ancestor of hers who had founded Fort Swetenham in Malaya. We sometimes went for picnics to this uninhabited ghostly house set among deodar trees. Fanny described it in her memoirs as 'situated between a hill called "The Park" and "Ben Oge" with Bhadraj to the west. The situation is most beautiful - the hills magnificent and well wooded.' It was still like that in the 1940s. I and my friends would walk out there through the fine rhododendron forests with their crimson blossoms, Margaret being carried in a conical *khandi* on the back of a coolie and Michael riding a small pony.

In the cool of the evening we would usually go for walks around 'The Deodars'. On one side the road led steeply down the hillside through the woods to a deserted house, the garden of which was a riot of tiny yellow banksia roses. On the other side, a steep path dropped down to Fox's Hill, a ridge high above the old polo ground. Here grew wild flowers very like English ones, as well as yellow raspberries which the children loved picking. Years later when I was working on the careers of the artists, Thomas and William Daniell, I noticed in their diary that they too enjoyed wild raspberries on their trek from Hardwar to Srinagar (Garhwal) in 1789 and that they noted stinging nettles and other English wild flowers: daisies, dandelions, thistles, St John's wort and honeysuckle.

To Miss Swetenham and the old Anglo Indians I met in Mussoorie I owe interests which have dominated my life since my return to England. The house itself and its surroundings gave me a background to my work on British artists in India. Unlike so many Anglo-Indians she was proud of her mixed ancestry. A number of her friends were of a similar type. Two delightful old Anglo-Indian ladies, the Misses Hearsey, lived in Dehra Dun and sometimes came to tea with her. Later I realised that they were the descendants of the famous old military adventurer Hyder Jang Hearsey, who in 1798 was ADC to the Nawab of Oudh and later served in the Maratha Wars. He accompanied

Moorcroft to Lake Mansarowar, and in 1808 assisted Webb in surveying the source of the Ganges. He had been given land in the Dun by the East India Company and it was there that his old descendants were still living. I have often wondered what happened to them after Indian Independence when these estates were all confiscated by the Indian Government. Another interesting Anglo-Indian visitor at 'The Deodars' was Captain Skinner, a descendant of the famous James Skinner, Colonel of the 'Yellow Boys', the Irregular Regiment formed by him. It was from his descendants that in 1960 the India Office Library was able to acquire the 'Skinner Album' with its fine miniatures by Indian artists of Skinner's Horse in their yellow uniforms and portraits of many of Skinner's old Delhi friends. In 1989 when I was last in India I attended a service in Skinner's church one Sunday in Delhi and met the present Colonel Skinner there who looks astonishingly like his ancestor. As a result of these 'hotweathers' in Mussoorie I came to value these old Anglo-Indian families and appreciate their many special qualities. The information they gave me has subsequently helped me to identify the subject-matter of many of the paintings, engravings and writings with which I have since been involved, especially the aquatints of the Daniells, and those of James Baillie Fraser who painted and published the first views of the Himalayas.

While I was there I saw much of our old collector friend of Patna days, PC Manuk and his companion Miss Coles, who were staying at the Savoy Hotel during the hot weather. Manuk was very frail and rarely went out but Miss Coles would often stroll along the Mall and call on me at 'The Deodars'. She was a gaunt figure with her well-tailored grey suit, grey toque and neatly rolled umbrella, looking more like a lady walking down Bond Street than a woman out for a stroll in the Himalayas! Miss Coles was very bitter about the Europeans in Patna as they completely cut her and 'PC' socially. The reason was that Miss Coles had originally been employed as a companion to look after Manuk's wife who had become mentally ill and eventually had to go into an asylum in England. Miss Coles had then stayed on and devotedly looked after old 'PC' for the rest of his life.

23

War and the Troubles

But dominating this peaceful life in the Hills in 1942 was news of the War and the political troubles in India. The constitutional proposals of Sir Stafford Cripps made in 1942 had been rejected. The All India Congress Working Committee in a meeting in Allahabad in April 1942 had discussed Gandhi's draft resolution which said that 'the proposals showed up British imperialism in all its nakedness as never before, that the British were incapable of defending India and since Japan's quarrel was not with India, the British should therefore withdraw from India.' (AE Bion, *Police Report* 'Administration of the Police in the Province of Bihar for the year 1942' Govt. Printing 1943) At Wardha in July, however, the Working Committee passed another resolution which differed in one respect from Gandhi's Allahabad Draft: Congress agreed to the temporary stationing of Allied troops in India to repulse Japanese attacks. In May, Dorman Smith, the Governor of Burma had flown out to India. During that summer, British troops on leave from Burma began to arrive in Mussoorie in large numbers. During May news had reached us of the retreat of civilians from Burma through the Tamu Pass. In June the first of these refugees - a doctor, his wife and two small children - arrived at 'The Deodars' and I gained first-hand news of the horrors they had experienced.

Gradually the doctor's wife began to speak to me about their trek. She described the heart-rending moment when they were ordered to leave their home at Maymyo. She looked sadly back, she said, as she went out through the garden gate and saw the verandah with their children's tricycles and toys in their usual place, looking quite normal, knowing that she would never see that house again, that she had lost everything she possessed except her family and feared that they too might not survive the problems she guessed would lie ahead.

She described how they had walked out of Burma over the mountains carrying their children, struggling up tracks deep in mud, soaked by the monsoon rain, through dripping forests, assaulted by leeches, mosquitoes and sand-flies. They had slept at night on the ground under bits of rag tied to branches of bushes. They contracted dysentery and fever. It was terrible, she said, to hear their children shrieking out at night in their sleep. But they had struggled on and just managed to reach India where help awaited them.

In that same summer of 1942, a group of strapping, handsome, bearded British soldiers began to arrive in Mussoorie. They were in great demand from the memsahibs for dancing at Hackman's and the Charleville Hotel! These were the Chindits, Orde Wingate's men, who were waiting to be sent into Burma, to the area south of Myitkyina, to support Stillwell's advance.

Meanwhile on the Plains there was trouble of another kind. Throughout India, as the Police Report for 1942 pointed out, 'There had been an abnormal increase in the cost of living, staple foods and other commodities. The influx of refugees from Burma, the general unsettled state of the people due to the threat to India from Japan produced a marked effect on the crime situation. Offences against property, particularly dacoity, assumed serious proportions. By the end of the first half of the year, the crime situation was critical and then in August came the call from Congress for civil disobedience all over India.'

Towards the end of July, while I was still in Mussoorie, I suddenly ceased to receive my daily letters from Bill, and it also became clear that the newspapers were being censored. One must remember that at this time there were serious issues at stake. The Japanese were on the borders of India, ready to invade, and it was essential that communications across India had to be kept open for the rapid movement of British troops. For three weeks in August I received no letters from Bill, and then at last he wrote to say that I could safely return with the children. I at once hurried back by train and was met at Patna station by Bill with a bodyguard of two plain-clothes police and three Gurkhas.

That evening after the children were in bed, Bill began to tell me about the troubles in Patna. At the beginning of August he had been told to arrest the Congress leader, Rajendra Prasad (later to become the first President of India). Bill already knew him well. On going to his house he found him in bed with fever, so he asked Government for orders. He was told to get a medical report on the seriousness of his condition. The Civil Surgeon came, examined Rajendra, and reported that he had only got a mild recurrence of malaria, and could safely be moved. So Bill went personally to his house and Rajendra came out leaning on his arm. By this time it was pouring with rain and the car would not start! Bill called on the onlookers to give a push, but having recognised who was being arrested, they not unnaturally refused. Bill and the Civil Surgeon themselves had to get out and push. The engine started, they jumped in and sped off to the gaol.

Then the Prime Minister of Bihar, Sri Babu, also had to be arrested. Bill called at the house of Sarangdhar Sinha, where the Prime Minister was staying. Sarangdhar (the father of the little girl I had coached in Ranchi) explained that Sri Babu was out down the bazaar, but would be coming back at lunch time. 'Would you tell him', said Bill, 'to get his things together and I will call back at about three o'clock for both of you.' So they too were quietly arrested and taken off to gaol. Bill then checked up on all the other important politicians: Sarangdhar explained that Anughra Narain Sinha was away from Patna and Jagat Narain Lal was in Bombay. The other politicians were on a second list, so there were no more to be rounded up that day. Bill regularly visited the political prisoners in gaol to see that they were well and not too uncomfortable. Rajendra was bored and said he would like some novels by Pearl Buck, an author whose work he greatly enjoyed. Bill borrowed a few for him from the European Club Library. Sarangdhar complained that the butter was rancid. Butter was in short supply during the War, so Bill sent him some of ours.

The All India Congress Committee members who were not arrested, framed a 12 point programme which included 'the disobeying of all orders by Government-servants or soldiers, the non-payment of Government revenue, the activising of the masses by the students, and the adoption of all non-violent means to paralyse the administration'.

Throughout July, Bill told me, tension had been gradually mounting but during the second week of August, following the arrests of the most prominent politicians, the situation in Patna rapidly deteriorated. On 10 August crowds of students began to march in bands, to demonstrate and stop cars. Government officers from the suburbs, such as Kadam Kuan, were being threatened and were reaching their offices with difficulty. They had to leave their cars and often change out of their European dress. Mr Creed, the Deputy Inspector General of Police, moved down from the New to the Old City to direct operations, as the local Superintendent of Police was ill with fever and the Additional Superintendent was a gentle Kayasth. How could these officers bring drive and energy to a force which lacked cohesion, had no heart and was already looking beyond the immediate struggle to the leaving of the British and the return of a Congress Government with fresh powers? The tactics of the movement were fast becoming apparent - to break morale, to tell the British to quit, to sap their resistance. 'That night', Bill noted, 'Creed came round and we discussed the position.' Resistance was now widespread and no mere demonstration. As long as defiance was individual, resistance could be held, but that was changing and was no longer possible.

On 11 August the students began to march in even larger bands, blocking traffic and shouting slogans, '*British Raj nicche ho*' (Down with the British Raj), '*Inqilab Zindabad*' (Long Live Revolution). They gathered first at the Girls' High School. Although the gates were shut, girlish voices shouted slogans from within and the students answered from the road. Then they marched and gathered in a vast crowd at the far end of the Maidan, planning to occupy the Secretariat. A small group of police, already there, held them off for a while, telling them to disperse, but the police were mere cyphers. The students stood firm, chanting '*Gandhiji ki jai*' (Long Live Gandhi). More students and still more joined them. The huge crowd then surged forward. The thin line of police was completely overwhelmed and the crowd rushed shouting towards the Secretariat, threatening to burn it down. The danger was clear. Not only was the building a symbol of British government: it housed the Land Records of the whole province. Bill attempted to talk to the crowd, but to no avail. It was then as a last resort that he ordered the police to open fire on the mob. This was the saddest day of Bill's whole career in India, for eight students were killed. That night BN Dey, the Superintendent of Police, rang Bill up saying that he was sending down to the house a bodyguard of two plain-clothes police and three Gurkhas; 'They will get you if they can', he said. It was this group that had met us at Patna station on our return from Mussoorie.

A large number of arrests were later made, and camp gaols had hastily to be set up. The first night after the firing, at half-past ten, Bill had a telephone call from the Gaol Superintendent, saying that the prisoners were still at large in their temporary barbed wire enclosures. It was long past lock-up time, but they were refusing to go into their wards. The Superintendent had been arguing with them for three hours; he had even tried beating them, but the angry crowd still loitered outside, and would not go in. He had decided that he must open fire, but in order to get Magisterial permission, he asked Bill to come down to the gaol to approve the action.

Bill drove quickly to the gaol. He noted in his diary 'The night was moist and the air soft and chilly. At the gaol the electric lights were like huge pallid eyes looking down at the stormy scene below. The gaol warders were standing in greatcoats with their rifles ready, and further back in their prickly barbed-wire enclosures, the prisoners either stood in groups or strolled listlessly beneath the stars. From time to time they shouted slogans, breaking the silence with roars of sudden hate.'

'When I went inside,' Bill noted, 'the Superintendent asked me if he should open fire. I said, 'Not yet, I will first ask the prisoners to go in.' Then I started a long walk through the lines and cages of barbed wire. At every shed, I stopped and asked the prisoners why they were not inside. Then they aired their grievances about the conditions. They had complained again and again, they said, but nothing had been done. There was not enough water, there were too few latrines, the roofs leaked, the sheds had sodden floors, there were not enough blankets, the hospital was too small, and many of the sick lay heaped together on the ground. I talked to them quietly. I said I would come down again the next morning and see what could be done to improve things but that meanwhile they must go inside. By now it was almost midnight. The air was blowing cold across the plain. Realising that they had gained their point and that I had listened to their complaints, the prisoners sullenly agreed to go in and the warders locked the gates.

First thing next morning, I drove down to the gaol again and walked among the prisoners. It was then that I saw the camp gaol in all its squalor - the frail sheds, the sagging barbed wire, the filthy tin latrines. The crisis had come upon us too quickly for anything to be properly organised or planned. The huge enclosures had just sprouted.' This was undoubtedly the saddest period of Bill's official career.

24

'The Ever-Singing Santals'

At the end of 1942, we heard that Bill was to be transferred from Patna to Dumka as Deputy Commissioner of the Santal Parganas. It was a long drive from Patna to Dumka so we decided to stop on the way for a break at Bhagalpur and have lunch with Gordon Ray, an ICS officer there who had been at Oxford with me. At this time he was in charge of the Bhagalpur Gaol where a number of political prisoners, including some who had been arrested in Patna, were being held. Over lunch Gordon suggested that we should visit one of these prisoners. She was, he said, a delightful intelligent young Parsee woman who had been arrested in Patna during the troubles: he had been trying to make her as comfortable as possible, but she was terribly bored. Gordon took us to her cell. He had given her a bright striped Swat blanket for a bed-spread and a tiny piece of ground adjoining her cell where she could do a little gardening and grow a few flowers. Bill asked her why she had come to Patna at this particular time and she said she had been sent by Congress to investigate 'the atrocities of Butcher Archer', and she had been arrested on arriving. She had clearly not caught our name on being introduced by Gordon! We soon got talking. On hearing her surname 'Narojee' we guessed that she came from the well-known Bombay Congress family and it emerged that she was in fact 'Bul', an old friend of Verrier Elwin, about whom he had often spoken to us in the past. Gordon had to enlighten her as to our identity. We noticed that she had copies of *Time and Tide*, to which she subscribed. She lent these to us and we in return lent her several copies of the *New Statesman* which we regularly received from England and which we happened to have with us. I hope these exchanges helped her to be a little less bored during her confinement. Such were some of the strange contradictions of the political scene in India at that time.

Many years later, when we were back in England, we were involved in another similar episode. One evening Natwar Singh, the Indian High Commissioner rang Bill up to say that the Congress Minister, Jag Jiwan Ram,

Krishna and the milk-maids - stealing their clothes while bathing
(Santal painting, Jadupatua scroll)

was in town staying at the Westbury Hotel. He very much wanted to meet Bill again. Bill said he was not aware that they had ever met. 'Oh, yes you have', laughed Natwar. Shortly afterwards an official car arrived at our house in Hampstead and took Bill to the hotel. Jag Jiwan Ram then explained how in the hot weather of 1942, he was arrested in Patna and was among a group of political prisoners who were being transferred to the Ranchi Gaol where Government had decided it would be cooler for them than in Patna. They were all lined up on the railway platform and a platoon of British soldiers had been deputed to see them on to the train. Jag Jiwan said that the soldiers were hustling them rather roughly when a young Englishman in a topi came up and said, to the soldiers, 'Leave these gentlemen to me. I will see them on to the train.' When they were all seated, Jag Jiwan asked the other prisoners in the compartment, 'Who was that young man?' and they replied, 'Oh, don't you know him? That was WG Archer, the Collector of Patna.' Jag Jiwan Ram said that Bill had then walked round the train asking them if they were comfortable and whether they had any problems. He had never forgotten that incident and had always wanted to say 'thank you' personally. As Bill got in the car ready to return home, a chaprassi rushed up and thrust a large tin of Indian Nescafe through the open window on to Bill's lap. The next day we saw in the newspaper that there was an acute coffee shortage and that the price of Nescafe had shot up in England. The prudent Jag Jiwan Ram had clearly come to London forewarned and well prepared for all eventualities. He was repaying his debt to Bill in a very typical way!

Our posting to Dumka was perhaps for us, as a family, the happiest period of all our time in India. Set in the midst of beautiful wooded country with an aboriginal population - the Santals, it was certainly the most comfortable posting we had ever had. We had a delightful old bungalow. It had large spacious rooms with French windows opening on to a wide verandah, which encircled three sides of the house and was so wide that the children could play there on wet days in the Rains and dash around on their tricycles.

We were surrounded by our faithful servants, most of whom had been with us for many years. There was Iltaf, the Muslim driver, with his purdah wife and their son. His relation, Nathun, was the *kitmatgar*, a gentle reliable man. Sudhan, the cook, was a gentlemanly old Hindu, assisted by his casteman Gulab Chand, the *panikala* and *masalchi*. Adwardhan whan, the bearer, had now retired and his place had been taken by Manohar, a tribal Uraon. I can never forget the loyalty and efficiency of this team who moved

The old Dumka bungalow

WGA and MA at Dumka, 1943

around with us over the years and gave us continual comfort and support, sometimes during difficult times, as in Patna during the troubles of 1942. Most beloved of all was Lakhan, a Santal, the chief *chaprassi*, a man of many parts who was learned in Santal lore and life. The children adored him: he could make dolls and toy bullock-carts out of bits of wood and bamboo and weave grass fish-traps and baskets. One year he built for the children a little mud house in the garden where they could eat their meals and play. As pets we had Ramaswami the cat, Kalu the dog, Brownie the pony, and for a time, a pet deer, Bambi. Others such as mynahs and rabbits, came and went, but usually met some unfortunate end. Michael became a great favourite with the Santal *chaprassis* who would take him out before breakfast to set his fish-traps in the paddy fields and accompany him on walks and visits to neighbours in the evenings.

In front of our bungalow was a large tank, around which were grouped the houses of the various officers and a few European residents. On one side lived the Superintendent of Police, Mr Maguire, and the Additional Deputy Commissioner, Mr Bhagat. The latter had a purdah wife and several daughters. From visits to them I came to learn much about the problems of a joint family and a purdah household with lively intelligent daughters under the thumb of an uneducated mother with very limited interests. On the opposite side of the tank lived the subdivisional officer, Syed Muhammad Naqavi, a Muslim, also with a purdah wife who was extremely clever with her needle, making elaborate stuffed dolls, one of which she gave to Margaret. Next door to us lived Mrs Robinson, the widow of an estate Manager who had recently died. She could not return to England because of the War and the cessation of passages for civilians. She had green fingers and raised beautiful flowers in her garden and the hanging baskets on her verandah. Behind us lived the Gausdals, dour Norwegian missionaries of the Northern Churches, but kind and devoted friends. Nearby lived a wealthy Calcutta businessman, Manilal Nahar. Apart from these neighbours and some of the office clerks the population was entirely Santal.

Now that the children were bigger, they could happily tour with us in tents and accompany us to villages where they were a great source of interest. Michael soon became involved in his father's enthusiasm for tribal welfare. It was easy to recognise a Santal village where morale was high, as there would be a neat *manjhithan* in the centre - a thatched shed in which the spirit of the village was believed to live. If the *manjhithan* was broken down, Bill would sometimes upbraid the headman. Michael, having listened to these

Michael, aged 8 and Margaret, aged 5, outside their own Dumka house, 1945

Our nanny, Mariam (a Christian Santal) with Margaret at Dumka, 1945

conversations, on one occasion himself took the headman to task for the ruinous state of the *manjhithan*! Some months later, we revisited the village and found a new neatly-built *manjhithan* and round the barge-board were engraved in Santal the words 'Erected by order of the Baba Michael.' We have often wondered what future anthropologists might make of this inscription! Will Baba Michael perhaps be seen as a godling?

Touring in the cold weather in tents was a great delight. We would breakfast in the morning outside the tent and in the evenings light a huge bonfire. It was then that the villagers would come in from miles around to sing and dance for us and Bill would collect much information about the Santals which he later published in *The Hill of Flutes* (1975). In this relaxed atmosphere, local problems could be discussed and Bill could make enquiries about Santal law which he was attempting to record. As a magistrate, he had soon discovered that there had been many miscarriages of justice in the past, very largely due to ignorance of Santal law and custom on the part of Hindu officials and British District Officers, and he felt that justice could only be done in the Santal Parganas if cases in which both parties were Santals were settled by Santal law.

Eventually Government came to appreciate the problem and Bill was put on special duty from 1 June 1945 to codify Santal law. He set up 20 centres where young Santal-speaking officers could check and cross-check by interrogation the draft material he had collected. It soon became clear that there was an excellent body of Santal law accepted by all Santals throughout the district. Tribal law was in many ways socially far more advanced by modern standards than Hindu or Muslim law. Santal women, for example, had far more civil rights. Bill became especially interested in the ceremony of 'bitlaha', an impressive form of punishment for incest which was seen as threatening to destroy the integrity of the tribe. Bill suggested the setting up of tribal courts in tribal areas to administer tribal law. He worked tremendously hard and produced a massive report which systematically codified Santal tribal law. However Independence followed in 1947, and I doubt if the report will ever be used now to bring greater justice to the Santals themselves, who, I understand, along with many other tribal people, have been callously neglected by the Indian Government since the British left.

During the time that this report was being prepared, the verandah was filled every day with groups of Santals, usually the headman or elders of the tribe who came in to testify to their customs. A loyal band of officers carried out the arduous work of attestation. It was a most happy, stimulating and rewarding period.

MA with Michael, Margaret and Mariam, crossing a river in a 'donga' made of hollowed-out tree trunks joined together, 1945

However the War was now over. Michael was eight years old and it was clear that he must go to school and start a European education. He had already had an English governess in Dumka and then went to Woodstock, an American co-educational school at Mussoorie. Transport was now beginning to return to normal. We had already arranged for him to go to the Dragon School at Oxford, so in October 1945 I went ahead with the children to settle both of them at school. Margaret went to a little boarding school, Annisgarth, in the Lake District. I stayed in a small hotel in Oxford, where Bill joined me when he came home on leave in 1946. Meanwhile, as a result of the reputation Bill had gained as an authority on tribal affairs, the Assam Government asked for him to be lent on his return to the Naga Hills. Philip Mills, the Governor's Advisor on tribal affairs in Assam, had asked the Bihar Government to release him, so Bill set off in 1947 to go to Assam to work among the Nagas. Meanwhile, I stayed behind for a little while longer in Oxford to see that the children had settled down and it was here that I wrote and published my first small book on *Patna Painting* (1947) which was still fresh in my mind.

25

Return to India by Flying Boat

By July 1947 the children appeared to have settled down happily in their schools and I had made arrangements for their summer holidays. I felt I could now return to India. This time I went not by ship but by flying-boat. I noted in my diary after arriving in Calcutta: 'I can hardly believe that a week ago I was queuing for vegetables in war-time London and today I am back in Calcutta in a different world where the old pre-war values and comforts still persist.'

In the Customs at Karachi I realised I was indeed back in 'India'. There was all the bustle and muddle which I love and which was such a relief after the drab looks and silence on the English suburban train of a week ago. There was a lively discussion of Sind's economic position while we were waiting for the suitcases to be loaded onto the coach, and a Parsee official announced that 'we, like the British, can now stand aloof and look at it all from the outside'. I enjoyed their description of a rich Marwari who last week smuggled in vast quantities of sterling hidden in a basket of fruit and how the coolie dropped it at the crucial moment in the Custom House revealing all. And it was comic to see a Muslim grannie protesting violently as a female official hurried her to the 'Ladies Room' to have her ample skirts ransacked.

I reached the hotel in Karachi just as the brilliantined sahibs and their hard-faced wives were sitting down for their short-drinks before dinner. A group of British civilians waiting for a York plane to England that night were sitting beside me and their conversation was a ridiculous caricature of the British in India. They gloatingly foretold civil war in two months, with Russians swarming down through the Khyber and India unsafe for all women and children.

The next morning I left in a Dakota for Calcutta. We had elevenses at Jodhpur near the pink palace. In the restaurant sitting over coffee a wealthy Hindu businessman told me how he was hastily selling his property in Sind, and a Hindu provincial civil servant anxiously related his fears for the future:

'How can I, a Hindu, hope for fair promotion within Pakistan!' Soon we were banking round the two Delhis, the one a maze of mosque, Red Fort and bazaar, the other white and immaculate with its ordered houses and gardens, one a symbol of an 'empire' that had long ago ended, the other of an empire about to end. I listened over drinks to the typical gossip of how Indian civil servants were trying to squeeze themselves into this or that new post. There would be the new High Commissioner's Office, with possible new openings in the Foreign Service. There would be Trade Commissioners and new departments. Even the former clean wish for Independence seemed inseparable from place-seeking and intrigue.

The next day was all cloud with bursts of early monsoon rain, the clouds occasionally opening to give a view of the red soil and dark green forests of the Chota Nagpur plateau. I passed the time talking to my neighbour, an Indian girl, who was on her way to Santiniketan. She had been spending the holiday with Achariya Kripalani, the Congress President, who had just seen her off at Delhi, and she had been there in the midst of a conference with the Congress leaders. She was revolted by the accounts she had heard of the Bihar, Calcutta and Lahore killings but she would not admit that partition seemed the only answer. Her attitude and that of a Muslim businessman seated nearby were so utterly opposed that it made one despair of any solution. But it was pleasant to discuss Santiniketan with her and to talk about the artists Jamini Roy and Nandalal Bose. The latter was now in charge of the Kala Bhawan or Art School there and had endeared himself to all his pupils. He never missed the students' birthdays, she told me, and always sent them a small painting as a present. I noticed Aldous Huxley's *Limbo* lying on her lap. The clouds had now closed round us and I saw no more until we suddenly cruised past Howrah Bridge, the river shining like silver. In another few minutes we landed and I could see Bill waiting for me at Dumdum.

114

26

Calcutta: The Troubles

July 8, 1947

Bill and I had spent four days in Calcutta. We avoided a big European-style hotel and went to stay with our 'orthodox' friend, Gopi Krishna Kanoria in his Calcutta House. He was a Hindu banker and dealer in oil and grain but had a passion for Indian miniature paintings and Hindi poetry, especially that of Tulsi Das. Here in Calcutta, Gopi and his family lived on the first floor of a great tenement which was wholly owned by him. It was approached by a narrow dirty gully always full of sacred bulls. At the door you pushed them out of the way and then went upstairs in a slow lift. Each floor opened onto a central well with an iron railing running round all four sides. One could stand there and, like the warder of a gaol, see what every family on every floor was doing. Saris were hung out to dry on the railings like huge coloured flags, and the children scurried from floor to floor by the lift to play together. We kept seeing knots of them playing and peeping at us. By the end of our stay they had become brave enough to chase each other through our bedroom and out the other side.

Like the houses of so many wealthy Indians, it was a mixture of orthodox Indian and European gadgets: the marble bathroom was full of chromium taps, showers, soft soap containers and porcelain basins, but on the window sill lay a pumice-scraper for ceremonial bathing. We ate our food with our fingers in orthodox style off brass trays, but our tea was served in a magnificent English porcelain tea-set. Most of the beds were Indian string charpoys, but Gopi's wife proudly showed us her Vi-Spring mattress and large mahogany dressing-table.

We had arrived in Calcutta at a critical time. With the separation of India and Pakistan only three days away, communal tension had suddenly flared up again and yesterday was considered the worst day since the 'August killings' of '46. When we reached Howrah Station, we had had the greatest

115

difficulty in getting a taxi. No Hindu driver would go through a Muslim quarter and vice versa. The coolies, who always chatter like starlings, were huddled in gesticulating groups with frightened eyes. Police strutted in and out of the crowds, armed truck-loads of British soldiers were sweeping by, and all the shops were closed because of a strike. At last we found a taxi with a Hindu driver who was willing to take us to Gopi's house for an extortionate fare. As we raced along, we saw people rushing into their houses leaving the roads empty and silent. The driver muttered that there was a 4 pm curfew and we were already late. There was something sinister about these empty streets in this great city. Only a solitary sacred bull was wandering down the middle of the road. The scene reminded me of a Chirico painting of lonely squares and vertical buildings with death lurking round the corner. Suddenly a jeep of armed police zoomed down the road looking for stragglers.

When we reached Gopi's house, the shutters were bolted and barred, scared servants popped out with lurid stories of bomb-throwings and stabbings, while the children with excited eyes reported more and more dead in the street. That evening and all through the night, conch shells sounded their melancholy note, spreading panic and terror through the suburb. Just as even now a siren makes a Londoner's heart miss a beat, so, after the August killings, the sound of a conch shell evoked memories of fear and horror.

The next morning, Gopi's wife showed me their strong-room where all their valuables were now locked up for fear of the theft and pillage which usually accompanies communal trouble. She proudly showed me boxes of saris - chiffon, georgette and crepe-de-chine embroidered with seed pearls, also Benares brocades, heavy with gold and silver - all of them fairytale materials. Then we went out to do some necessary shopping, but with the exception of a few large English stores, all the shops were closed. It was a pathetic sight to see the great city at a standstill like this and I was glad to set off that night for the Naga Hills.

27

Naga Interlude

Although we spent only a few months there, it was an unforgettable experience, utterly different from anything I had previously known.

We began the journey to Assam by train from Calcutta. We crossed the Brahmaputra river by paddle-steamer, and then continued again by train. At dusk the next day we were dropped off at Nakachari in Assam for the night, and the next morning we set off on foot for the long 40 mile trek to Mokokchung. Naga porters with conical baskets on their backs had already gathered at the bungalow to carry our luggage. We set off early and started to march through densely wooded country, the hilltops rising out of the morning mist like islands in a white sea. The jungle grew denser and denser with a tangle of creepers, bamboos and tree-ferns. Mauve orchids clung to the branches. On the way village headmen in their scarlet blankets came out to welcome us with gifts of a chicken, a pineapple or a few eggs. Their bamboo houses on the hillsides were poised on stilts, the verandahs jutting out in front over the steep hillsides. At last on the fifth day we reached our headquarters at Mokokchung. Our house was a small wooden bungalow on a steep hillside with superb views of the mountain ranges and deep valleys around us. On one side was a small tea garden and on the other a vegetable garden and an orchard with bananas, pineapples, chestnuts, plum and peach trees. The house has been described by a whole line of scholars and administrators including JH Hutton and Philip Mills who had earlier lived there. The next morning village officials gathered at the house and talk immediately began through the interpreters ranging over the recent political developments and the coming changes. Some of the Nagas wanted a separate State with complete independence from India, others wanted to remain part of Assam in the new India. Meanwhile administration had to continue as normal.

Constant touring in the old way followed and we visited in turn the various Naga tribes who lived in the administered area - the Angamis, Lhotas, Kalu Kenyus, Sangtams, Imchungras and Rengmas - who all had their own

To the Naga hills in Sankalamba's 'kundi' (basket), 1947

distinctive dress, artefacts, architecture and languages. All the villages were set amid superb mountain scenery. All had 'bachelors' dormitories' where the boys lived until marriage. The distinctive wooden housefronts were decorated with carvings recording the number of wild buffaloes (*mithan*) sacrificed and the number of human heads taken by the owner on various raids. Each of the villages had a huge log-drum where the spirit of the village resided. Everything including the bamboo *'chungas'*, the everyday bamboo and wooden drinking vessels, were decorated with distinctive carving celebrating the sacrifices and achievements of the owner. The wooden sculpture on the housefronts and the village gates also recorded the prowess of the village and its inhabitants showing the number of heads taken on raids or the number of *mithan* or cocks that had been sacrificed by the owners. Gradually we began to recognise the various styles of carving which differed from tribe to tribe. Beyond this administered area to the east lay the unadministered territory with its huge hills tumbling into Burma.

In our own bungalow compound were the houses of the various Naga 'interpreters' each representing a different tribe, each with a separate language but communicating with Bill through Naga-Assamese. These village officials accompanied us on our tours to the different linguistic areas.

Headman of Helipong and MA drinking rice-beer, 1947

119

Sangtam Naga girls and MA, 1947

Dancing at Tuensang, Chingmei (Chang), 1947

120

In the course of our first tour we visited Bill's superior officer, the Deputy Commissioner, Sir Charles Pawsey, at Kohima. It was here that the Japanese invasion of India had been halted in June 1944. About a thousand British troops had been huddled in shallow trenches when the Japanese attacked Kohima and the seige lasted for thirteen days. There were heavy casualties. The great cemetery is now cared for by the War Graves Commission and it has been beautifully preserved like those in Europe.

Everywhere in the villages were tallies of the heads taken by the various tribes and everywhere there were stories of the war and the hated Japanese with their wanton killing not only of the Nagas but of the fish in the rivers and the animals in the jungle.

The longest and most exciting tour we made was across the eastern frontier to the Kalu Kenyu tribe in order to bring this new area, which had been giving trouble, under administration. Differences in the way of life were evident as soon as we crossed the boundary. Even the appearance of the villagers changed - they became more unkempt and wild, their long hair knotted on the nape of the neck and they had great 'ostrich plumes' tattooed on their chests. We camped there for several days. One day a band of warriors from a remote village suddenly came rushing into our camp to meet Bill - the new Deputy Commissioner, a dazzling sight with their brass ornaments glittering in the sun, hornbill feathers and scarlet plumes of dyed goats' hair tossing as they ran. There was a great stampede with clashing *daos* and jingling brass ornaments on their chests as they danced for us. Their cloths were embroidered with patterns of cowries, the tallies of heads they had taken. Round and round the proud line of warriors paraded, shaking their tasselled spears, thumping their black hide shields and chanting their wild songs and dirges. We knew this was the swan-song of a culture doomed in the modern world.

Meanwhile there was constant talk of Independence and the coming changes. There was a fear amongst the administered Nagas that the tribal area would once again become turbulent as soon as the British left. In August 1947 Indian Independence was announced and Bill's career in the Indian Civil Service came to an end. He stayed on until early the next year but had to return to the administered area and then to England. The posting had been a thrilling finale to our years in India. I hear from the few people who have recently visited the Naga Hills that our fears were fully justified. Conditions there are indeed chaotic and the Nagas are still resisting the new administration and the political changes. We left India with great sadness, not knowing what career lay ahead for Bill who was only forty years old.

121

28

New Beginnings

In February 1948 I had had to leave the Indian Civil Service but had found
it hard to reconcile myself to life in England. I had spent over sixteen years
in India and with every year I had felt more and more that it was to India that
I belonged. I delighted in the Indian seasons. An 18th century resident, James
Forbes, had written, 'As a contrast to the violence of the monsoon and the
unpleasant effects of the hot winds, there is sometimes a voluptuousness in
the climate of India, a stillness in nature, an indescribable softness which
soothes the mind and gives it up to the most delightful sensations.' This was
my own experience and whether it was the winter, the hot weather or the rainy
season, I had found each month a source of novelty and stimulus. I did not
mind the heat. In fact it was the Indian sun, Indian warmth and Indian colour
which exhilarated me. For the greater part of my service, I had been a District
Officer in Bihar - unvigilated (except at long range), free (within broad limits)
to act as I liked and above all, with a positive role to play in Indian life and
society. I was responsible for law and order - for seeing that life went
smoothly - but even more, for the general welfare and happiness of the people
around me. In many of my postings, I had been the only Englishman for miles
around and I had therefore come to depend on Indian company for friendship,
talk and relaxation. I had found fulfilment in merging myself with the local
people. Together we would resolve problems, devise and carry out projects
and in the process I would go deeper and deeper into Indian life and customs.
Another 18th century visitor, Mrs Eliza Fay, had remarked in 1780, 'There
is something in the mild countenances and gentle manners of the Hindoos that
interests me exceedingly'. I too had felt this interest and whether it was with
tribal Uraons and Santals or Bihari Brahmins, Rajputs, Kayasths and Ahirs,
I had acquired a sense of Indian identity.

It was hardly surprising, therefore, that when I reached England in May
1948, bought a house in Oxford and tried to settle down, I was lost and
unhappy. It was not only the character of the English weather, its dull

depressing greyness, it was the lack of spaciousness, air and quiet, the rasped nerves of English city-dwellers, the aloofness of those around me, English reserve and lack of involvement. It was soon borne in upon me that I could not do without India and that if I was to be moderately happy, I must preserve, maintain and revive the Indian connection.

To reach this stark conclusion was easy but was there anything I could do? When India became independent in August 1947, the Indian Government declined to re-employ any British members of the Indian Civil Service. The decision was harsh yet, in fact, it was not unreasonable. India must not only be free but must be seen to be free, and if British officers were still in the administration, how were the villagers to understand that the British Raj was really over? Continuation in the ICS was therefore out of the question. But if the ICS was ruled out, what other job in India was possible? I had no head for business. Indian taxation was severe. I could hardly live in India on my pension alone. I also had a son and daughter to educate. Everything pointed therefore to a job in England. Was there any occupation which would make England bearable also, at the same time, relieve my itch for India?

My first instinct was to consider full-time writing. For eight months I would be on full pay and this would be followed by a further period on half pay. The sums I would receive would not be large but they would see me through two years and in that time I believed I could sort myself out. Throughout my stay in India, I had felt a need to write. Pressure of official work, involvement in district affairs and the tensions of the war had often made writing impossible. But from time to time I had written poems and had translated tribal and popular Indian poetry. Some of these translations had been published in *New Verse, Contemporary Poetry and Prose* and *The Listener*. I had published two books on the poetry of the Uraons - *The Blue Grove* and *The Dove and the Leopard* and a third book *The Vertical Man* on primitive Indian sculpture. I had done a little reviewing for *The Listener* and even contributed some scraps of journal to *Longman's Miscellany*. I had also been interested in primitive and modern art and although I had written next to no art criticism, I was more than alive to its possibilities. I had acquired quantities of material about the primitive sculpture of the Naga Hills. I had become fascinated by Indian miniatures. I fancied, also, that granted the time, I had quite a story to tell about my whole experience of India. If I took Indian culture and poetry as my subject, I argued, I had the example of the Chinese scholar, Arthur Waley; if I took art-criticism and art-history, there was Herbert Read and if I chose Indian life as a whole, there was a precedent in

Maurice Collis. Maurice was particularly apposite since like myself he had been a member of the Indian Civil Service. His career had lain in Burma but in my own time Burma had still been run by ICS officers and I myself had even placed it second in my order of preference after I had been accepted for the service. Substitute India for Burma and our cases were virtually identical. Maurice had saturated himself in Burma and had then retired to England. He had become a full-time writer on Eastern topics and had availed of his Burmese experiences in order to bring them to life. Moreover, he had a strong feeling for art. He was keenly interested in the contemporary scene and for many years was art-critic for *The Observer*. He also collected Chinese ceramics and modern paintings. His career, I thought, provided an instructive parallel, for if Maurice could become a full-time writer and art-critic, I flattered myself that I could too. Writing about India could never be the same as actually living there but it might, to some extent, relieve my sense of unintended alienation. It would make the break less painful and provided I could come to terms with England, I might yet get through.

Such reasoning had a facile plausibility. But I had overlooked important factors and among them was myself. That I wanted to write was certainly true. But except when I was 'seized' by a poem or was under the stress of an examination, I had always found writing difficult. The final product might be smooth, clear or vivid, but the actual process was agonising in the extreme. Instead of knowing, at once, the right approach to a chapter or an article, I would be faced with several alternatives. I would try one after another; draft would succeed draft but despite the most strenuous efforts, clarity of thought and logic of arrangement would elude me. I would feel stuck and furious with disappointment - howling, as it were, at my own impotency - I would succumb to frenzied despair. For many writers, Harold Macmillan's dictum - 'cool, calm deliberation solves all problems' - may well be true but in my own case, feeling warred with thought and the result, as often as not, was a devastating sense of fatuous stupidity. It was clear that the adroit and business-like manner in which Maurice Collis addressed himself to writing was beyond me and that compared with my other master, Herbert Read, I was also sadly deficient. Herbert was later to write, 'My advantage is that when I write, I write without fuss or hesitation, rapidly and enjoyably. I concentrate quickly and in almost any surroundings. Without this lucky faculty, I could not have accomplished half my writings.' Obviously I did not have this lucky faculty and since I did not I might as well give up.

The results can be anticipated. For a year I moped in Oxford, striving to complete a book on the Santals - the largest tribe in Eastern India - whose poetry I had collected and translated. At the same time I collaborated with Roland Penrose and Robert Melville in the first great exhibition launched by the Institute of Contemporary Arts, *40,000 Years of Modern Art*. This assignment took me to many museums, enlarged and quickened my responses to painting and sculpture and enormously widened my comprehension of modern art. It was to prove a liberal and far-reaching education for which I shall always be grateful. But in one sense it confirmed my fears and suspicions. The catalogue to the exhibition involved the writing of an introduction. Robert Melville did part of it and I did the rest. But for both of us it was a taxing strain. When at last it was finished I returned to my Santals, only to discover that from sheer fatigue, I had reached a dead-end. The lesson was plain. Occasional writing might be possible but the profession of full-time writer was out.

It was at this juncture that an alternative presented itself. During short home leaves from India between 1939 and 1946, I had visited the Indian Museum in Imperial Institute Road, South Kensington. It was actually a department of the Victoria and Albert Museum ('V & A')- its 'Indian Section' - but since it occupied a separate building some three to four hundred yards from the main Museum and was in a different road, it was often thought of as an independent institution. I had come to know its Keeper, K de B Codrington and although I did not share his relish for Indian archaeology, prehistoric beads and village handicrafts - still less his allergy to painting - I warmed to his enthusiasm for India. He had been born and brought up there and his attitude to the country was not unlike that of Kim. When he went to India, he would slip quietly 'underground' and although he would surface from time to time to meet friends in high places, he preferred above all to sun himself in the Indian village. In 1926 he had produced a gigantic volume on *Ancient India* and a little later a revised edition of Vincent Smith's *A History of Fine Art in India and Ceylon*. In 1947 he had helped to organise the Royal Academy's great exhibition of Indian Art, the first of its kind to be held in England. Codrington had chosen the stone sculptures, bronzes and minor arts and had written about them in a little symposium, *Indian Art*, published before the exhibition and in the monumental catalogue which was published later. I had arrived in London in May 1948 - too late to see the Exhibition - but I had met Codrington in the autumn and winter of that year and in the spring of 1949. My little book on primitive Indian sculpture had appeared in 1947 just before the exhibition and had been sold at the Royal Academy's sales counter. To Codrington I must have seemed a keen, if inexperienced, art-investigator as odd in my own way as he was in his. But I had one redeeming feature, a similar attitude to India. It was this, I think which enabled him to view me as an ally and supporter. He gave me his warm approval and his forceful backing was shortly to ease my problem.

In the early summer of 1949, there came a sudden piece of news. Codrington had completed a stage in his restless journey. He had been appointed Professor of Indian Art and Archaeology in the University of London. His post was vacant and in the chaotic improvisations of post-war Britain it was suggested to me by John Irwin that I should apply for the post. Irwin was a young and recently appointed Assistant Keeper in the Indian Section. We had met briefly in India when, as a result of an injury in the War, he had been appointed an ADC to the Governor of Bengal, Sir Richard Casey and we had developed a warm if fitful friendship. In 1949, he was 32 - too young to be considered for the post himself but with an eye to the future, anxious not to be blocked by too young or permanent a senior. Leigh Ashton, he told me, was anxious to appoint him but could not do so for the present. It would suit everyone, he said, if I could have the post for about ten years since, after that, he would be ten years older and hence able to assume charge.

The proposal, I confess, was not at first sight, very congenial. I had utilised museums but not admired them. I connected them with the obsolete and the moribund. They were mausoleums and the prospect of even a temporary career in the gloomy galleries of the Indian Museum did not exactly thrill me. But I realised that my future was unsettled. I could hardly support my family on an ICS pension. I would eventually need regular employment. If I applied for a ten-year contract, it would doubtless be renegotiable and if after ten years I had had enough, I could leave and thus regain my freedom. Appointment on a permanent basis was impractical since I had taken the compensation granted to members of the ICS for loss of service. Any member accepting a permanent pensionable post under the British Government - and appointment at the 'V & A' was such - was not allowed to accept compensation and if already taken it would have to be refunded. My own compensation had been exhausted by buying a house in England. Refund was therefore impossible. Yet assuming I had somehow realised the money and repaid it, did I really need a permanent post and would I not be losing more by forfeiting this capital sum for a second long-delayed pension? Service in the ICS had brought me extremely meagre financial gains and with next to no savings the capital sum was not to be lightly refunded. To have a 'temporary' post in the 'V & A' might in such circumstances be no bad thing. But could I stand it? Had I the right qualifications? Although I was not a 'permanent' writer, I still wanted to write. Would Museum life promote or stifle writing? As I pondered these matters, I realised yet again that the answer must lie in myself.

A museum is basically a collection and although far from large, our own collection of Indian miniatures and folk paintings had made me aware of what collecting meant and how one should proceed. Problems connected with our own collection had begun to intrigue me; and as if in unconscious anticipation of a museum career before leaving India I had made a trip round northern India in March and April 1948, visiting the larger museums and photographing pictures. I already knew the leading Indian scholars and connoisseurs and some of the dealers. With all of these I had had long discussions and had exchanged opinions on dates and attributions. I had also become aware of all the information and gossip about styles and schools which circulated by word of mouth. It was this 'gossip' which created current ideas of 'schools' - often erroneously but at times correctly. I had discussed and listened far more than I had read but without this grounding in Indian chat, how could a beginner have got his bearings? As I bore in mind this stock of 'subterranean' knowledge, my sixteen years saturation in India, my three small books already published and my study tour of Indian museums, I could see I was not unqualified for the post. But did I want it? John Irwin did his best to reassure me. Museum life, he said, was by no means arduous. One could do almost what one liked. Hours were flexible. One could go to exhibitions. The lunch hour was infinitely extendable. 'Codrington', he added 'was hardly ever there'. He was convinced I could easily complete my Santal book in Museum time. Everyone did his own writing in Museum time... delusive visions danced before me. But more than anything else I saw that the post would have one inestimable advantage. It would keep me in daily touch with Indian culture, Indian art, Indian objects, Indian ideas, Indian things and Indian people. India would once again be my work and life. The job itself would ensure a vital connection. I decided to apply and, to my great astonishment, I was eased through the competitive interview by Codrington himself. Ebling, from the Ministry of Education, Leigh Ashton, Codrington and a member of the Civil Service Commission were the interviewers and I was to learn later that there had been no serious rival. A day or two later Codrington rang up. 'I am happy to congratulate you', he said. There was a gap of a few weeks but by May 1949, I had been formally appointed Keeper on a ten years contract and on 15 June I took up the position.

My first six months went in taking decisions. To make the Indian Section a true art museum - to bring it into line with the new 'V & A' under Leigh Ashton, there would clearly have to be a purging of redundant materials. Boards of Survey comprising myself, John Irwin and a Keeper from another Department were therefore set up and group after group of objects was examined and scrutinised for retention or disposal. Once a Board had made its recommendations, they went to Leigh Ashton, as Director, for approval and thence to the Ministry for confirmation. Wherever possible we found alternative institutions to take the discards. The result was a great clearing of the air and as the true art collections came steadily into view my spirits rose and I felt buoyant and exhilarated. I began to live again, if not in India, at any rate at only one remove from it. I was surrounded by Indian works of art. It was my job to think about them.

The Indian Section, as I now experienced it, was not at all what I had imagined it. That perhaps, was only to be expected in the light of post-war confusion. But even before the War, it had been a vast depository of bric-a-brac. International trade exhibitions had come and gone and each had left behind it a deposit of models, samples, industrial contrivances and ethnological specimens. A life-size plaster cast of a first century gateway from the Buddhist stupa at Sanchi towered into the roof. A great house-front from Ahmedabad greeted you as you entered. There was a huge collection of Indian shoes. Even Queen Mary had amassed over the years a formidable array of nineteenth century wooden carvings, mica paintings, ivory knick-knacks and rhinoceros horns, and since Buckingham Palace had no room, there it all was. Of sculptures, bronzes, textiles and miniature paintings there was certainly an important nucleus. But it was obscured by mountains of rubbish. The acquisition registers were fairly up to date, but the finding lists were unreliable. None of the collection had been fully catalogued and many pictures had not even been mounted. There was clearly a great deal of 'weeding out' and conservation to be done.

'Weeding out' was to dominate in various ways the next two years. But alongside it was a fundamental problem which I saw I must quickly solve. It was perfectly true, as John had assured me, that one need not do much work. But that was not the point. Unless one worked at it, the post would have no meaning. As a District Officer in Bihar, I had realised that nothing short of total involvement in the affairs of one's district would do. Begrudge time, hold oneself back and the job went sour. To make life at the Museum worthwhile, I must identify myself with all that the Museum stood for. But

WGA with John Wiltshire, Senior Museum Assistant at the V&A India Dept, in 1960s

what, in practice, did that mean? A Keeper of the Indian Section was supposed to know all about Indian Art, be able to answer every question and provide all exhibits with scholarly labels. But was this humanly possible? The Academy's great exhibition of 1947-8 had shown how complex and varied Indian Art was and how every branch of it bristled with problems. Torrents of new material were appearing. It would take years to get on top of them. And if one did, what then? To appreciate Indian Art one must understand Indian culture, literature, poetry, history and religion. Some of these subjects one might master but surely not all. Codrington had known about some things but nothing at all about others. Only one conclusion was possible: specialisation was unavoidable. But on what should one specialise and on what should one not? That was the problem.

The answer was provided partly by my own history and interests and partly by events. In Indian bronzes, other than tribal or village, I had little interest at that time and to Indian sculpture - with certain major exceptions - I was lukewarm. For this there were several explanations. My own India, Bihar, had few great temples and little sophisticated sculpture in situ. To see such sculpture one had to go to a Museum, but in Bihar, there was only one museum at Patna, and in Bengal the only museum of substance was the Indian Museum at Calcutta. In both these museums were ranks of sculpture but for very few of them could I muster much enthusiasm. It was true that the Patna Museum possessed one great masterpiece - a female figure from Didarganj. Standing some four feet high it was conspicuous for the glossy polish of the sandstone, its sumptuous majesty of physique and the eager radiance of the face. The flat haunches contrasted strangely with the narrow waist, great hips and hugely rounded breasts. It was the epitome of early India and was dated to between the 2nd century BC and the 2nd century AD. In the Indian Museum at Calcutta, there was a semi-circle of railing pillars from the Buddhist stupa or relic-mound at Bharut. These contained a number of figures in relief - most of them female and with the same kind of rhythmic assurance. They also were early Indian and dated from perhaps the 2nd century BC. If all Indian sculpture had been like the Didarganj figure and the Bharut railing figures, how strongly I might have been tempted to specialise on sculpture, but the majority of Indian sculpture was not and although the photographs of Raymond Burnier were beginning to reveal the glories of Khajurao, such medieval carving was far from typical of Indian sculpture as a whole. During my service in India I had seen only two great sites, the 'Black Pagoda' at Konarak in Orissa and the cave-temple of Elephanta on an island off Bombay. Each had its own powerful aura and it was obvious that to appreciate the sculptures fully one should see them in their original settings. For the rest I knew Indian sculpture only from photographs and these were normally of such a dullness that I winced when I looked at them. To specialise on sculpture from a desk in the Indian Section struck me as futile. Admittedly the Section possessed two radiant female figures of about the 2nd century AD from Mathura. There was also the famous Sanchi torso - decapitated, armless but very beautiful. But there was little else. The sculpture collection was not to be ignored - it was one of the few considerable collections in the West. But it was not a great collection and although in the last 25 years, significant pieces had been added, it was still far from comprehensive. If one wanted to specialise on Indian sculpture, one would have to do so in India itself.

There remained Indian painting and here the Museum's collection was particularly strong, and rapidly expanding. Shortly before I had joined the Museum, part of the private collection of PC Manuk and Miss GM Coles, the devoted couple whom I had known in Patna had reached the Museum by bequest. Another private collection - that of Sir William Rothenstein - was to be acquired a year or two later. Both collections were strongest in paintings from the Punjab Hills. There was thus a great deal of material on which to work. Moreover the Royal Academy exhibition of 1948 had revealed some vital new evidence. Yet little had so far been done to differentiate styles, attribute them to particular states and establish fixed dates. The Punjab Hills themselves, 300 miles long and 100 miles wide, lay east of Delhi and Lahore. They were bounded by the Punjab Plain on the south and west and by the Himalayas on the north east; and until the 19th century they had included not less than 35 different feudal states. These had been explored in a desultory sort of way but little that was definite had as yet emerged. It seemed likely that almost every state had had a local style of painting but which of the many different styles belonged to which state was still a mystery. Hundreds of pictures from the area had been trickling out and reaching museums and collectors. While in India I had often heard labels such as 'Kangra', 'Garhwal', 'Jammu' and 'Basholi' applied to certain pictures but when one asked why, it was rarely that one got a proper answer. 'Kangra', 'Garhwal' and 'Jammu' were the names of three large states, 'Basholi' that of a small one. Everyone knew - or thought they knew - what 'Kangra' painting was. It was connected with a smoothly flowing line, a special type of serene and lovely female face and an atmosphere of courtly poetry. Yet 'Kangra' pictures were very far from all being the same. What then *was* Kangra painting? How had it developed? Which paintings were precursors? Were there other courts besides that of Kangra at which 'Kangra' pictures had been painted? Questions such as these had been seething in my mind from long before I joined the Museum but I had had no time or opportunity to resolve them. Now they could no longer be avoided. The Manuk and Coles pictures - and later the Rothenstein ones - must soon be catalogued and as a prelude to cataloguing, some attempt at reconstructing these local schools must be made. How best could this be done? It seemed that my role at the Museum must be in the field of painting.

The weeks and months that followed my appointment were among the most exciting and stimulating of my life. While still in India, I had had few opportunities for sustained reading. The little country towns in which I lived had no libraries of the type I required. Prior to the war, I had sometimes had books posted to me from the Imperial Library, Calcutta. But the war came, administration became daily more arduous and complicated, one worked longer and longer hours. Back numbers of journals and magazines were inaccessible and so scholarly reading came to a halt. Once I had joined the Museum, the scholar came into his own. The 'V & A' has the National Art Library and there was hardly a single book or journal dealing with Indian Art which it did not have. *The Journal of the Indian Society of Oriental Art, The Journal of Indian Art and Industry, Rupam, Roopa Lekha* - journals which were hard to come by in India were all there, and I could look them up at will. As for Indian religions, history, life and culture, the India Office Library in Whitehall had a seemingly inexhaustible stock of books. If the V & A failed there was the 'IOL' which almost always could supply me with what I needed.

With such facilities at hand, I could broaden and deepen my knowledge. I read voraciously. I turned, for example, to books on sculpture so that knowing next to nothing about it, I could soon broadly distinguish different styles and periods. I learnt from books the attitudes to life which were endemic in ancient and medieval India and thus the India which I thought I had known so well in the 30s and 40s took on an added air of ghostly grandeur. It was necessary too to investigate Indian religion more carefully. I had acquired a rough idea of what Vishnu and Shiva stood for but I knew very little mythology and had still to master the full story and significance of so important an incarnation of Vishnu as Krishna. Yet it was ridiculous to 'enjoy' Indian miniatures, especially those from Rajasthan and the Punjab Hills without knowing who were the chief protagonists and why they had been portrayed. In picture after picture Radha and Krishna appeared. But in fact who was Radha? Why had Indian love poetry taken the form it had? Why should India have its own Song of Songs? Why should Radha, a married milkmaid be Krishna's principal love and why should Krishna end his life on earth as a feudal magnate with many wives? To such questions I did not find the answers at once. But the quest had its own exhilaration and in filling out my knowledge I was educating myself in still further aspects of India.

For Indian art the years 1949-1970 stand in sharp contrast to the years 1916-1948. Not only was there a great expansion in public and private collections, thus providing more materials for study, there was also a new approach to evidence and a determination to place the subject of Indian painting in particular on sounder foundations. 'Opinions' whether by dealers or scholars were no longer viewed as of great account. 'Facts' were in every way more important. Indeed as research progressed and the small band of scholars slowly increased in numbers, none of the work by any previous investigator appeared sacrosanct. It was seen that not one but many types of evidence were needed for establishing local schools of painting. Where evidence existed it must be tested. Where it was wanting, it must be sought. No factors which might possibly assist in identification should be left out and in order to locate and date one style it would be necessary to date and locate all styles. It was on building up the Museum's collection of paintings and on attempting to identify the different schools that I therefore decided to concentrate.

The years that followed at the 'V & A' were full of interest and excitement. Although the Indian Section at that time was away from the main Museum building in Exhibition Road (it did not move to the main building until 1955), one was nevertheless constantly meeting one's colleagues from other Departments. There was Arthur Lane of Ceramics with his clear and brilliant mind steeped in the Classics. There was James Laver, Brian Reade, Jonathan Mayne and Arthur Wheen. From these learned scholars I obtained constant stimulus. The result of these contacts was first of all the production of a small monograph *Indian Painting in the Punjab Hills* (1952). It had no great pretension - it was rather a jeu d'esprit, an experiment in detection which I hoped might end some of the prevailing confusion. I conceded that there was not much evidence to go on, but evidence of a kind did exist. There were portraits of known people, pictures with inscriptions and pictures of known provenance. Oral tradition had also in certain cases, been recorded. If one patiently sifted the material and assembled what evidence there was, clues to origin might well be found and some of the problems might be solved. Eventually I published *Indian Paintings from the Punjab Hills* (1973).

In this little book, I had made a start in identifying local schools of painting in the Punjab Hills and also in giving an overall view of the subject. As was to be expected one or two Goliaths in the subject dismissed me as a small insignificant David. Others such as JC French, NC Mehta on the other hand gave me warm and generous encouragement. Although I was a newcomer to the field, they felt I had none the less made some useful points and they were pleased to find a much younger writer continuing their pioneer efforts.

The next unexpected repercussion, however was to follow a year later in 1953. Apparently some months after the publication in 1952 of my *Indian Painting in the Punjab Hills*, copies had reached New Delhi and it was there while browsing in one of the bookshops in Connaught Circus that MS Randhawa chanced to light upon it. Already interested in painting he was devoted to the Kangra Valley on account of its people and the beauty of the scenery. He was intrigued to find a book which dealt not only with his favourite part of the Hills but also with its painting. He quickly bought a copy and rushed through its pages. As he digested it he realised that stimulating though my book might be in its discussion of the different schools of painting it was obviously only a beginning. The materials were scanty and he realised how handicapped I was by never having been to Kangra. He wondered whether even now the final answers to many of my problems might still be in the Kangra valley itself. JC French had met descendants of Kangra artists. Were they still alive? If so, what could they remember? To realise that questions of this sort were still unanswered was for Randhawa a sort of challenge. He decided to track down as many local collections as he could, photograph the pictures, record family and local traditions and in a word, test my conclusions on the spot. For almost a year he went on quietly doing this. Then in May 1953 he decided to write to me. On 26 May his airletter, dated 19 May 1953 reached me as I sat in my office in the Indian Section. It was addressed from the Commissioner's House, Ambala. It bore the sender's name 'M.S. Randhawa, ICS Commissioner's House, Ambala Cant, Punjab, India'. I had no idea who Randhawa was and as I carefully slit the letter open, I experienced curiosity, surprise and even some anxiety. What had I done? I quickly got in touch with MS Randhawa and a deep friendship with him soon developed which resulted in numerous return visits to India, staying with him and his family at Chandigarh and in many delightful treks in the Himalayan Hill states with him, where we examined the collections, met the rulers and discovered which artists they patronised. Gradually it became clear that there

134

WGA being presented with a Sikh sword

had been painting in more than thirty Hill States each with its distinctive style - Arki, Bhagal, Bangahal, Bandralta, Bushahr, Basohli, Bhadrawah, Bhadu, Bhoti, Chamba, Chanderi, Datarpur, Garhwal, Guler, Hindur, Mandi, Mankot, Nalagarh, Nurpur, Jammu, Jasrota, Jaswan, Kahlur, Kangra, Kotla, Kulu, Siba, Simur, Suket, and Tirikot which we were gradually identifying. In all of these small states artists obtained patronage from the rulers, some giving lavish patronage which produced massive collections of paintings. Our many tours throughout this most beautiful part of India were a constant delight.

The hospitality of Randhawa and his wife was most generous and my wife and I spent many cold weathers in their house at Chandigarh meeting other scholars and connoisseurs. It also led to our friendship with Aijaz-ud-din of Lahore who was greatly interested in Sikh painting. This latter friendship led to the discovery of the Sikh relics and Lord Dalhousie's collection at Hadington, East Lothian, and the eventual return of the Sikh relics to Pakistan. This interest in Pahari Painting became all consuming and resulted in my two volume catalogue *Indian Paintings from the Punjab Hills* (1973). It was the happiest period of my life.

29

The India Office Library and Records

In 1954 the Librarian of the India Office Library rang up Bill to say that, in addition to the 'Johnson Collection' of Indian miniatures, he believed the India Office Library also possessed 'a few miscellaneous Indian paintings'. He wondered whether Bill could find time to catalogue them. The work, he imagined, would only take a few weeks at most. Bill replied that unfortunately he was too busy with his new job at the 'V & A', but he thought his wife might be able to help.

A few days later I arrived at the old India Office Library in King Charles Street, off Whitehall, where Stanley Sutton was waiting for me with a small pile of tattered albums containing Indian 'Company Paintings'. Mr. Sutton apologised that there was no vacant room where I could work, but there was a small room with a sink and a gas-ring where the staff made their tea. It was empty most of the day, so I was given a stool and I set to work cataloguing the paintings on the draining-board. The paintings mainly depicted the castes and tribes of India, and their occupations.

The task was finished in a few weeks. It then struck me that this was a rather meagre collection of paintings for such a famous library to have acquired in the course of one and a half centuries. But no-one seemed aware of any further paintings. I therefore began to prowl around the long line of rooms adjacent to the Reading Room. Poking in corners, opening cupboards and climbing up ladders, I soon discovered numerous dusty brown-paper parcels as well as many unidentified portfolios. They all contained drawings and engravings made mainly for the British by both British and Indian professional painters. There were drawings on paper and mica, from centres such as Delhi, Murshidabad, Patna, Lahore, Tanjore, and Trichinopoly. There were also five large and dusty volumes containing drawings by Chinese artists at Canton depicting Chinese drama, houses, villages, gardens and flowers. One large parcel, containing drawings of Java collected in 1811-13 by India's first Surveyor-General, Colin Mackenzie, was up a chimney keeping the soot from falling.

MA with Robert Skelton working on an India Office catalogue, 1959

I then turned my attention to the 'Iron Room' where the printed books were stored. They were shelved on iron mobile racking which ran on rails suspended from the ceiling - an invention which when it was installed in 1867 was the acme of modernity. Armed with a torch, I crept between the dark racks, peering for any volumes which might possibly contain drawings. Sure enough, a number came to light. I found 27 large volumes containing natural history drawings which had been despatched to the East India Company by Marquis Wellesley between 1798 and 1804. These contained 2,660 drawings of the flora and fauna of India. A number of collections in the Iron Room proved to be related to miscellaneous drawings in the corridor rooms. Three great volumes of Thomas Horsfield's Java drawings made between 1805 and 1819 related to several portfolios of Java in the corridor. Similarly, James Burgess's 16 volumes of archaeological drawings, made under his supervision in 1874 to 1890, had become separated from 79 miscellaneous drawings. There was also the splendid collection of miniatures collected in India by Richard Johnson (1753-1807). These paintings were either loose in portfolios or guarded into old albums.

My investigations proved a threat to life and limb since if the 'Paper-Keepers' (as the Repository Assistants were then called) set the racks careering along the rails, I was in danger of being squashed. On the days when I was known to be working in the Library, a cry would go up 'Are you inside, Mrs. Archer?'

It soon became clear that the Library's collection of paintings had for long aroused little interest. The Library had been mainly used by historians and linguists working on Sanskrit, Persian and the Indian vernacular languages. The paintings had been neglected and regarded as of little importance. Fortunately when dusted down or freed from their sooty wrappings, most were in sound condition. The mice, which had been happily nesting in another portion of the Library, had mercifully not reached the area I was exploring. Nevertheless, bindings needed to be renewed and drawings needed to be individually mounted. Stanley Sutton was anxious that the whole collection should be properly conserved and in 1954 lent it to the Indian Section of the 'V & A' where my husband arranged for the paintings to be cleaned, mounted and boxed.

While cataloguing these collections, I found gaps in series which at first seemed inexplicable. I then realised that some of the finest prints and drawings had been removed during the second half of the 19th century and framed for rooms in the old India Office (now the Foreign and Commonwealth Office). Until the second World War, the India Office had been a proud establishment, its main rooms elegant with fine furniture, oil paintings, watercolours and prints. I can remember how the lift-men would sit polishing their brass and would keep a rose or carnation in the vase beside the lever. By the mid 1950s, the situation was very different - the building was over-crowded, the Durbar Court filled with prefabricated buildings, and the staff were no longer concerned only with India. An attempt was therefore made to bring back the pictures which had come from the Library's collection and to reunite them in the appropriate series.

As a result of Indian Independence and the great Burlington House exhibition of 1947-48, a renewed interest in Indian painting had been rapidly developing. It was essential that the pictures should be conserved so that they could be safely handled by the growing numbers of students and visitors who now wished to examine them. During the years since Drs. Randle and Arberry had first listed the miniature paintings in the early 20th century, great strides had been made in the study of Indian painting. It was no longer useful to divide miniature paintings into 'Islamic' and 'Hindu' as they had first done. Robert Skelton was therefore sent by my husband to recatalogue the mini-ature collection, which was eventually published, with the help of Toby Falk and myself.

It was clear that a separate Prints and Drawings Section was needed so that all the original drawings, whether British or Oriental, could be brought together in one place. When the India Office Library moved to Orbit House, Waterloo, in 1967, this was at last achieved. Through pressure from Stanley Sutton, the post of a part-time Assistant Keeper was sanctioned, to which I was appointed. The new accommodation, with specially designed drawers and cupboards, enabled the prints, drawings and photographs to be system-atically arranged. The cataloguing, begun by me in King Charles Street, continued rapidly. Thus an almost unknown collection of grubby parcels and portfolios has been transformed into a superb collection, which is constantly consulted by students and scholars. As for myself, the two or three weeks that I expected to spend at the India Office Library extended themselves to 25 exciting and stimulating years, which have dominated the second half of my life.

Postscript

by Giles Eyre

The return of the Archers to England did not break their links with India, nor did Bill decide to rely on writing as a profession like Maurice Collis when he returned from Burma. What intervened was a friendship with Kenneth Codrington, Keeper of the Indian Section of the V & A. They had much in common and when Codrington was appointed Professor of Indian Art & Archaeology in the University of London, his job in South Kensington became vacant.

John Irwin, formerly ADC to Sir Richard Casey when he was Governor of Bengal, encouraged Bill to put his name forward. Not a Civil Servant, Irwin had already been recruited as Assistant Keeper on a permanent basis. But Bill's appointment in June 1949 was limited to a ten-year contract. Because of compensation and other terms of his severance from the ICS, Bill was precluded in theory - and as it turned out in practice - from taking on more than 'temporary' employment in his 'retirement'. He was only 42.

War-time conditions - and confusion since 1945 - had resulted in much of the V & A's huge and diverse collection being relegated to what was virtually a repository. To his surprise, Bill found not only important sculptures from Mathura and Sanchi there, but a remarkable collection of Indian paintings - many of which had not even been mounted. Of immediate interest to him was a recent bequest of works by Pahari artists from the collection of PC Manuk and Miss Coles, the devoted couple whom Bill had come to know intimately in Patna. This was subsequently to be augmented by the acquisition of the Rothenstein collection which was also strong in Pahari paintings. These miniatures from a secluded area in the Punjab Hills, about which there was little knowledge and much controversy, were to become a major preoccupation in Bill's research. Meanwhile, an overriding priority was coping with the entire contents of the collections under his care which were housed in the Imperial Institute. His first six months went in taking decisions chiefly based on his determination to make the Indian Section a fine art museum - to bring it into line with the new V & A under Sir Leigh Ashton. That Bill already knew the leading Indian scholars and connoisseurs, as well as certain dealers, was to be a significant factor in his success.

After supervising the move of the Indian Section from the Imperial Institute into the V & A building - itself an enormous task - he had time to rethink and reorganise the entire Indian Miniatures holding. He also bought much modern Indian art into the Museum. That he had a perspective above the conforming orthodoxy stimulated his staff. It was in his nature to encourage the young, and to take them into his confidence. In 1959, Bill became Keeper Emeritus - at first somewhat unhappy when John Irwin stepped into his shoes - but, as Bill wrote later to Cary Welch, "quite the best thing that ever happened to me. I had as good as completed my main contribution to the Museum, and - until 1967 when I retired at the age of 60 - I could concentrate on my research and art-historical writing. Since then, I have found the enforced 'leisure' of 'retirement'...... perhaps the most productive of my life."

Tim has related how, in 1954, she came to be put in charge of Prints & Drawings at the India Office Library & Records. She was to preside over them and her team for the next 26 years. Nevertheless, she would drop everything for her family and for Bill. Whenever she could, she would join him on his study tours in India. Their itinerary of a journey they made with Maurice Shellim to the South 'in the footsteps of the Daniells' was of special interest to me. This was partly the area that my Regiment had reconnoitred from Madras in 1942, when we expected that the Japanese would imminently land somewhere on the Coromandel coast. The Archers had never been there before and the deep Hindu south was an entirely new experience for them.

In 1966 I had travelled back to India for five months, at a time when I was aware that present publishing tastes and techniques were bringing Anglo-Indian and Indian art-historical subjects to a far wider public. Yet in the London salerooms there was still little interest in the work of European artists - however celebrated - who had travelled to the sub-continent from the late 18th century onwards. The Archers' original study of so-called 'Company painting' in 1955 - referring to the work of Indian artists for East India Company officials and other Europeans - was one of the books that I had taken with me to India. In my ignorance, I did not then realise that the IOL's collection of such was the largest and most comprehensive in the world.

It was shortly afterwards, in 1967, that the IOL & Records finally moved to Orbit House, across the river. Between then and 1980, Tim tackled this collection, publishing her *Company Drawings in the India Office Library* in 1972. In 1968, I had started up in Duke Street St James's, and it was not long before the Gallery held the first exhibition of similar examples we know of for sale. The commercial success of that particularly pleased Bill. It must have been about this time that I was first invited by the Archers to Provost Road. This charming house had wisely been bought by Bill when part of the Eton College Estate in Hampstead came onto the market. It was there that I was to spend many happy evenings. Only the tip of their collection was on the surface, so a discussion about attribution of any problem picture would often lead, after supper, to a session on the sitting-room carpet. By then it would have been strewn with transparencies, monochrome photographs and ephemera - rather reminiscent of the Berenson method.

The disciplines of authorship were central to the Archers' lives, and riddles of this kind were treated with as much enjoyment as seriousness. Bill was the instigator of disrespect for past opinions, while Tim's approach was initially more circumspect. They worked perfectly together as a team, both having a strong aversion to academic humbug. In the past, curators and others professionally involved with museums and libraries were not supposed to cohabit with dealers. Bill was a celebrated exception and was highly amused when I told him (after a visit to Paris) that I had approached curators at the Louvre and Musée Guimet in trepidation.

This was all of a quarter of a century ago, when Tim's welcome to me whenever I visited the IOL was so entirely different from my French experience. That was also true when I went to the States, where curators more often than not were private collectors - albeit in fields somewhat outside their professional commitment - and of those I came to know, many were originally introduced to me by the Archers.

In 1973 the American Federation of Arts funded an exhibition in New York which, largely thanks to Cary Welch, put down a marker for the importance of Indian painting during the British period. His catalogue *Room for Wonder,* was a model of its kind, and the exhibits relating to the years between 1760 and 1880 were exquisitely chosen. To those of us who were invited to New York it also marked the comparatively recent fascination cultured Americans had begun to feel for our oft-criticised colonial phase in the subcontinent.

In Cary's Foreword, he paid tribute to WG Archer and Mildred Archer:
"without the generous assistance and encouragement of both Archers,
I should not have dared venture into what I consider *their* territory."

It is now 14 years since Bill died, but it seems much less. The stature of certain friends tends to diminish with time, but not those who brought happiness with them. Bill was a many-faceted person, whom I can only remember smiling. He made a tremendous impression on me, not least because of the concentration of his will-power delightfully disguised by humour. But there is one characteristic which is historically indefinable - and that is charm. It was certainly not denied to Bill.

When Bill died, it seems certain that he was already confident that Tim's own scholastic career was on course. The two had always been complementary in their writing abilities, although it was Bill who much earlier had the driving compulsion to write. That she had the love and support of Margaret and Michael must have been of the first importance to her. But a new society was being born which did not have the same reverence for the left-wing thinking which had previously coloured her life. None of this she put down on paper, so to that extent her memoirs are incomplete. Tim already had a remarkable scholastic record, on which she could have rested. That was not her way, even if Bill was no longer there to take centre-stage. To a reader of these joint memoirs, the thought must occur that she intended them to be primarily a celebration of him.

Bibliography

W. G. Archer

Books:

The Blue Grove: the poetry of the Uraons (Allen & Unwin, London, 1940)

The Vertical Man: A study of primitive Indian sculpture (Allen & Unwin, London, 1947)

The Plains of the Sun [poems] (Routledge, 1948)

The Dove and the Leopard: more Uraon poetry (Orient Longmans, London, Calcutta, 1950)

Indian Painting in the Punjab Hills (HMSO, London, 1952)

Kangra Painting (Faber, Pitman, London, 1952; second and revised impression, 1953)

Bazaar Paintings of Calcutta (HMSO, London, 1953)

Garhwal Painting (Faber, Pitman, London, 1954; second and revised impression, 1955)

Indian Painting (Batsford, London, 1956)

The Loves of Krishna (Allen & Unwin, London, 1957)

Indian Paintings from Rajasthan (Arts Council of Great Britain, London, 1957)

Catalogue of an exhibition of works from the collection of Sri Gopi Krishna Kanoria of Calcutta, first shown at the Arts Council, London, 1957, and circulated in the United States by the Smithsonian Institute in 1958.

Central Indian Painting (Faber, Pitman, London, 1958)

India and Modern Art (Allen & Unwin , London, 1959)

Indian Painting in Bundi and Kotah (HMSO, London, 1959)

Indian Miniatures (Studio, London; Graphic Society, New York, 1960)

Kalighat Drawings (Marg, Bombay, 1962)

Indian Miniatures: From the Collection of Mildred and WG Archer, London [exhibition catalogue] (Smithsonian Institution, Washington, 1963)

Reflections of an Art Historian [convocation address] (Punjab University, Chandigarh, 1968)

Paintings of the Sikhs (HMSO, London, 1966)

Kalighat Paintings (HMSO, London, 1971)

Indian Paintings from the Punjab Hills 2 vols (Sotheby, London; Parke Bernet, New York, 1973)

The Hill of Flutes: life, love and poetry in tribal India: a portrait of the
Santals (Allen & Unwin, London, 1974)

Pahari Miniatures: A concise history (OUP, Bombay, 1975)

Visions of Courtly India: The Archer Collection of Pahari Miniatures
(International Exhibitions Foundation, Washington, 1976)

Tribal Law and Justice: A Report on the Santal (Concept Publishing Co.,
New Delhi, 1983)

Songs of the Bride: Wedding Rites of Rural India Edited by Barbara Stoler
Miller and Mildred Archer (Columbia University Press, New York, 1985)

Vernacular Articles:

Collections of Indian village and tribal poetry

Uraon	**Lil Khora Khekhel** by F. Hahn, Dharamdas Lakra and W.G. Archer, (Laheriasarai, 1941) - a collection of 2600 Uraon songs and 440 Uraon riddles in Uraon and Ganwari.
Ho	**Ho Durang** by W.G. Archer, B.K. Dutt and Ram Chandra Birua, (Patna, 1942) - a collection of 935 Ho songs and 400 Ho riddles in Ho.
Kharia	**Kharia Along** by Jatru Kharia, Daud Dungdung, Manmaeeh Totetohran and W.G. Archer (Ranchi, 1942) - a collection of 1528 Kharia songs and 446 Kharia riddles in Kharia.
Mundari	**Munda Durang** by Dilbar Hans, Samuel Hans and W.G. Archer, (Patna, 1942) - collection of 1641 Munda songs and 380 Munda riddles in Mundari.
Santali	**Hor Seren** by W.G. Archer and Gopal Gamliel Soren, (Dumka, 1943) - a collection of 1676 Santal songs in Santali.
	Don Soren by W.G. Archer and Gopal Gamliel Soren, (Dumka, 1943) - a collection of 1954 Santal marriage songs and cultivation songs in Santali.
	Hor Kudum by W.G. Archer and Stephen H. Murmu, (Dumka, 1944) - a collection of 492 Santal riddles in Santali.

Articles:

Contributions to **Man in India** during period of joint editorship with Verrier Elwin

Seasonal Songs of Patna District, xxii (1942), p233-237

A short anthology of Indian Folk Poetry: comment, xxiii (1943), p1-3

Baiga Poetry, xxiii (1943), p47-60

Santal Poetry, xxiii (1943), p98-105

An anthology of Indian Marriage Sermons, xxiii (1943), p106-110

Betrothal Dialogues, xxiii (1943), p147-153

Murder in Tribal India: comment, xxiii (1943), p179-181

An Indian Riddle Book, xxiii (1943), p265-315

Extracts from a Riddle Note Book, xxiii (1943), p323-341

Review of Bharati Sarabhai, 'The Well of the People', xxiii (1943), p350-352

Festival Songs, xxiv (1944), p70-74

Diwali Painting, xxiv (1944), p82-84

More Santal Songs, xxiv (1944), p141-144
The illegitimate child in Santal Society, xxiv (1944), p154-169
Folk-tales in Tribal India: comment, xxiv (1944), p207-209
Review of Verrier Elwin, 'Folk-tales of Mahakoshal', xxiv (1944),p 272-273
The Forcible Marriage, xxv (1945), p29-42
Review of Bishnu Dey and John Irwin, 'Jamini Roy', xxv (1945), p133-134
Rebellions in Tribal India: comment, xxv (1945), p205-206
Santal Rebellion Songs, xxv (1945), p207
The Santal Rebellion, xxv (1945), p233-239
Santal Transplantation Songs, xxvi (1946), p6-7
Sabai Cultivation in the Rajmahal Hills, xxvi (1946), p12-19
Tribal Administration: comment, xxvi (1946), p79-80
Tribal Justice: comment, xxvi (1946), p151-153
Two Kharia Weddings, xxvi (1946), p215-219
Ritual Friendship in Santal Society, xxvii (1947), p57-60
The Santal Treatment of Witchcraft, xxvii (1947), p103-121
Review of Stella Kramrisch, 'The Hindu Temple', xxviii (1948), p191-192
Review of Arthur Waley, 'Japanese Poetry', xxviii (1948), p192-194

Articles in Indian journals

The heron will not twirl his moustache, Journal of the Bihar and Orissa Research Society, xxix (1943), Parts I & II, p1-19

Marg   *Maithil Painting*, 3(3) (1949), p24-33
Some Nurpur Paintings, 8(3) (1955), p8-18
Problems of paintings in Punjab Hills, 10(2) (1957), p30-36
Survey of Rajasthani styles; Kotah, with William George, 11(2) (1958), p65-67
Review of 'Pahari Miniature Painting' by K. Khandalavala, xiii, No 2 supplement (1960), p1
Review of 'The Nala Damayanti Drawings' by A.C. Eastman, xiii, No 2 supplement (1960), p2-3

Indian Lit.   *Poet's Pictures: The Drawings of Rabindranath Tagore,* Indian Literature, Vol 4 (1961), p182-185
Lalit Kala   *Letter to the Editors,* No 8, 75 (1960, published 1962)
Roopa Lekha   *Paintings of India,* xxxiv, Nos 1 & 2 (1965), p63-75
A Tribute to M.S. Randhawa, xxxviii, Nos 1 & 2 (1969), p47-63
The Master of the Kangra Bhagavata Purana, xxxviii Nos 1 & 2 (1969), p64-72

Articles in various UK journals

Art & Letters *Sir William Rothenstein and Indian Art,* xxv, No 1 (1951), p1-7
R.S.A.   *Romance and Poestry in Indian Painting* [Sir George Birdwood Memorial Lecture], Journal of the Royal Society of Arts, Vol 105 (1957), p909-918
R.C.A.   *The Symbolism of Clouds in Indian Painting,* Ark 21, Journal of the Royal College of Art (1958), p33-35

The Listener *Reflections on the Kama Sutra,* lxix, No 1777 (1963), p665
Primitive Indian Sculpture, lxi, No 1554 (1959), p72
[And other journalistic items outside the mainstream of his work]

Prefaces and Forewords to books:

'Folk-songs of Chhattisgarh' by Verrier Elwin, (London, 1946)

'Kangra Valley Painting' by M.S. Randhawa (Ministry of Information & Broadcasting, New Delhi, 1954)

'Kangra Paintings of the Gita Govinda' by M.S. Randhawa (National Museum, New Delhi, 1963)

'The Kama Sutra' translated by Sir Richard Burton and F.F. Arbuthnot. Edited for first open publication. (Allen & Unwin, London, 1963)

'Love Songs of Vidyapati' translated by D. Bhattacharya. Edited with introduction, notes and comments (Allen & Unwin, London 1963)

'The Gulistan of Sadi' translated by Edward Rehatsek (for Burton and Arbuthnot). Edited for first open publication. (Allen & Unwin, London, 1964)

'The Koka Shastra' translated by Alex Comfort (Allen & Unwin, London, 1964)

'Indian Art from the George P. Bickford Collection' by Stanislaw Czuma (Cleveland Museum of Art, 1975)

WGA publications jointly with:

Robert Melville, **Forty Thousand Years of Modern Art** (Institute of Contemporary Art, London, 1948)

S. Paranavitana, **Ceylon: paintings from temple, shrine and rock** (Unesco World Art Series, Graphic Society, New York, 1957)

Edwin Binney 3rd, **Rajput Miniatures** (Portland Museum, 1968)

S. Paranavitana, 'The Sigiri Grafiti', **An Anthology of Sinhalese Literature** Edited by C. Reynolds, (Allen & Unwin, London, 1970)

WGA and MA jointly:

Santhal Painting in **AXIS** No 7, Quarterly Review of Contemporary Painters & Sculptors (1936), p27-28

Indian Paintings for the British (OUP, Oxford, 1955)

M. Archer

Books [while in India]:

> **The Bihar Reader** (A Primer and 5 Volumes), by M.E. Whitaker & MA - illustrations and maps by MA in some. (Khadgavilas Press, Patna, 1936)
>
> **Morris Atalanta's Race** Edited by MA in collaboration with S. Moinul Haq, (Khadgavilas Press, Bankipore, 1936)
>
> **Patna Painting** (The Royal India Society, London, 1947)

[on return to UK]:

> **Tippoo's Tiger** (HMSO, London 1959 and 1983)
>
> **The Daniells in India: an exhibition of water-colour and other drawings made by Thomas and William Daniell during their tours of India from 1786-1793** (Commonwealth Institute, London, 1960)
>
> **Natural history drawings in the India Office Library** (HMSO, London, 1962)
>
> **The Daniells in India, 1786-1793** (Smithsonian Institution, Washington, 1962)
>
> **Romance and poetry in Indian painting** [exhibition catalogue] (Wildenstein, London, 1965)
>
> **Indian miniatures and folk paintings from the collection of Mildred and W.G. Archer** [exhibition catalogue] (Arts Council, London, 1967)
>
> **Indian architecture and the British** (Hamlyn, Feltham, 1968)
>
> **British drawings in the India Office Library** Vol 1 Amateur Artists; Vol 2 Official and Professional Artists (HMSO, London, 1969)
>
> **Indian paintings from court, town and village** [exhibition catalogue] (Arts Council, London, 1970)
>
> **Company drawings in the India Office Library** (HMSO, London 1972)
>
> **Artist adventurers in eighteenth century India: Thomas and William Daniell** [exhibition catalogue] (Spink & Son, London, 1974)
>
> **Indian Popular Painting in the India Office Library** (HMSO, London, 1977)
>
> **India and British Portraiture: 1770-1825** (Sotheby, London; Parke Bernet, NY, 1979)
>
> **Early Views of India: the picturesque journeys of Thomas and William Daniell** (Thames and Hudson, London, 1980)
>
> **The tranquil eye: the watercolours of Colonel Robert Smith [of] a journey down the Ganges, 1830** (London, 1982)
>
> **Between battles, the album of Colonel James Skinner** (London, 1982)
>
> **The Marquis Wellesley Collection: Indian artists under British patronage** (London, 1983)
>
> **The India Office collection of paintings and sculptures** (The British Library, London, 1986)
>
> **Visions of India: the sketchbooks of William Simpson, 1859-62** (Alfalak/ Scorpion, London, 1986)
>
> **Company paintings - Indian Paintings of the British Period** (Victoria & Albert Museum, Mapin Publishing, 1992)

Articles:

British Patronage of Indian Artists: Sir Elijah and Lady Impey, **Country Life,** (18 August 1955), p340-341

Indian Paintings for British Naturalists, **The Geographical Magazine,** (September 1955), p220-230

Indian Mica Paintings, **Country Life,** (16 February 1956), p298-299

The Daniells in India, **Country Life,** (23 January 1958), p150-1

Archaeology and the British interlude in Java, **The Geographical Magazine,** (February 1958), p460-472

A Georgian palace in India: Government House, Calcutta, **Country Life,** (9 April 1959), p754-755

India and Natural History: the role of the East India Company, 1785-1858, **History Today,** (November 1959), p736-743

Forgotten painter of the Picturesque: Henry Salt in India, 1802-1804, **Country Life,** (19 November 1959), p890-891

Hunting with cheetahs, **The Geographical Magazine,** (March 1960), p485-492

The two worlds of Colonel Skinner, **History Today,** (September 1960), p608-615

Review of 'The Greeks in India' by George Woodcock: *The Hellenic Raj,* **History Today,** (September 1960), p655

The Daniells in India and their influence on British architecture, **Journal of the Royal Institute of British Architects,** vol 67 no. 11, (September 1960), p439-44

Chinese Lanterns, **The Geographical Magazine,** (December 1960), p452-457

Review of 'John Jacob of Jacobabad', by H.T. Lambrick: *Innovator in India,* **History Today,** (December 1960), p870-871

The Social history of the Nautch Girl, **The Saturday Book,** (1962), p242-254

India and Archaeology: the role of the East India Company, 1785-1858, **History Today,** (April 1962), p272-279

Indian Painting for the British, **Commonwealth Journal,** Vol. V No. 3, (May-June 1962), p141-143

India Revealed: sketches by the Daniells, **Apollo,** (November 1962), p689-692

From Cathay to China: the Drawings of William Alexander 1792-94, **History Today,** (December 1962), p864-871

Picturesque India with the Daniells, **The Connoisseur,** (March 1963), p171-175

Review of 'An Embassy to China: Lord Macartney's Journal, 1793-1794', edited by J.L. Cranmer-Byng: *Macartney in China,* **History Today,** (May 1963), p357-358

Company architects and their influence in India, **The Journal of the Royal Institute of British Architects,** (August 1963), p317-321

Mission to Burma 1855, **History Today,** (October 1963), p691-699

Birds of India: Christopher Webb Smith in India, 1811-42, **The Geographical Magazine,** (December 1963), p470-481

Indian Miniatures, **Art International,** (5 December 1963), p20-23

Georgian Splendour in South India, **Country Life,** (26 March 1964), p728-731

The East India Company and British Art, **Apollo,** (November 1965), p401-409

Indian art, **Emergent Nations,** (December 1965)

Domestic arts of Mithila: notes on painting, **Marg,** (1965), Vol xx, no. 1, p47-52

Painting in Bihar: Bazaar style, **Marg,** (1966), Vol xx, no. 1 p53-4

Review of 'South Asia: a short history' by Hugh Tinker: *India, before and after,* **History Today,** (November 1966), p801

Aspects of Classicism in India: Georgian buildings of Calcutta, **Country Life,** (3 November 1966), p1142-1146

British painters of the Indian scene (Sir George Birdwood Memorial Lecture), **Journal of the Royal Society of Arts,** Vol 115, (1967), p863-879

English gardens in India, **Country Life,** (2 November 1967), p1120-1123

Gardens of delight, **Apollo,** (September 1968), p172-184

Baltazard Solvyns and the Indian Picturesque, **The Connoisseur,** (January 1969), p12-18

Benares and the British, **History Today,** (June 1969), p405-410

British Painting in India, **Europe and the Indies: the era of the Companies,** 1600-1824 (BBC pamphlet, London, 1970), p28-32

Review of *European Architecture in India, 1750-1850* by Sten Nilsson: **The Art Bulletin,** Vol 52, (1970), p218-219

English artists working in India, **Arts Review,** (28 March 1970), p188-189

Company painting in South India: the early collections of Niccolao Manucci, **Apollo,** (August 1970), p104-113

The talented baronet: Sir Charles D'Oyly and his drawings of India, **The Connoisseur,** (November 1970), p173-181

Art of the East India Trade, **Arts Review,** (7 November 1970), p720

India, **Arts Review,** (5 December 1970), p795

Madras's debt to father and son: the work of John and Justinian Gantz, **Country Life,** (17/24 December 1970), p1191-1193

Banaras and the British, **Chhavi, Golden Jubilee Volume, Bharat Kala Bhavan, 1920-70** (Banaras, 1971), p70-74

Paintings for the East India Company, **Discovering Antiques,** part 65, (1971), p1549-1553

Arthur William Devis: Portrait painter in India (1785-95), **Art at Auction 1971-72** (London, 1972), p80-83

Tilly Kettle and the Court of Oudh, **Apollo,** (February 1972), p96-106

An artist engineer - Colonel Robert Smith in India (1805-1830), **The Connoisseur,** (February 1972), p78-88

Review of 'The Great Moghuls', by Bamber Gascoigne: *The Moghul Dynasty,* **History Today,** (February 1972), p147

Hills and forts of South India: the travels of the Daniells I, **Country Life,** (1 November 1973), p1370-1372

Architecture of Oriental Genius: with the Daniells in South India II, **Country Life**, (8 November 1973), p1454-1458

Review of 'A Concise History of India' by Francis Watson, *From Raj to Raj*, **History Today**, (June 1975), p443

Wellington and South India: portraits by Thomas Hickey, **Apollo**, (July 1975), p30-35

Renaldi and India: A Romantic Encounter, **Apollo**, (August 1976), p98-105

Review of 'Lucknow: the last phase of an Oriental Culture' by Abdul Halim Sharar *An Indian Glory*, **History Today**, (November 1977), p750-1

James Wales: Portrait painter in Bombay and Poona, 1791-95, Dr. Moti Chandra Memorial Volume, part I, **Journal of the Indian Society of Oriental Art**, New Series, Vol 8, (1977), p57-64

Review of 'The Orientalists' by Philippe Julian, **Journal of the Royal Society of Arts**, (January 1978), p111-12

Review of 'Much Maligned Monsters: a History of European reactions to Indian art by Partha Mitter (Oxford, 1977), **Apollo**, (May 1978), p439

Works by William Alexander and James Wales: Pictures of note by British artists in the collection of the Royal Asiatic Society, **The Royal Asiatic Society: Its History and Treasures** (ed. S. Simmonds and Simon Digby, Brill, 1979), p116-125

Colonel Gentil's Atlas: an early series of Company Drawings, **India Office Library and Records, Annual Report, 1978** p 41-45

Some reminiscences of the Prints and Drawings Section, 1954-80, **India Office Library and Records Annual Report, 1980**, p33-38

Review of 'The Classical Tradition in Rajput Painting from the Paul F. Walter Collection' by Pratapaditya Pal, **Journal of the Royal Society of Arts**, (April 1981), p313-4

Exotic Commissions: Sir Elijah and Lady Impey: collectors of Indian paintings, **Interiors**, (March 1982), p70-79

Review of 'India Discovered' by John Keay, **Apollo**, (March 1982), p212

Introduction to catalogue 'Thomas and William Prinsep in India', Spink & Son Ltd., (April 1982)

Company Painting at Eyre and Hobhouse, **The Burlington Magazine**, (June 1982), p372

Review of 'Views of Medieval Bhutan' by Michael Aris *Sublime Grandeur*, **The Literary Review**, (June 1982), p22

India Revealed: the aquatints of Thomas and William Daniell, **Hemisphere**, (Australia 1982) Vol 27 no 2, p72-77

Mr Cobbes' cabinet of curiosities, **Country Life**, (10 March 1988), p130-133

Forewords:

'India and the Daniells' by M. Shellim, (Inchcape/Spink, London, 1979)

Reprint of 'Bengal Obituary of 1851' (BACSA, Putney, 1983)

MA publications jointly with:

John Bastin, **The Raffles Drawings in the India Office Library** (OUP, Kuala Lumpur, 1978)

Toby Falk, **Indian Miniatures in the India Office Library** (Sotheby, London; Parke Bernet, NY, 1981)

Ronald Lightbown, **India Observed**, catalogue of the Victoria and Albert Museum exhibition for the Festival of India, London, 1982

C. Rowell and R. Skelton, **Treasures from India: the Clive collection at Powis Castle,** (National Trust/Herbert Press, London 1987)

Toby Falk, **India Revealed: the art and adventures of James & William Fraser, 1801-35** (Cassell, London, 1989)

🌴 🌴 🌴 🌴 🌴

For further details of their work, reference can be made to The Archer Collection in the British Library - Oriental and India Office Collections, MSS Eur. F. 236

Dr. William George Archer, OBE, MA(Cantab), D.Litt
Dr. Mildred Agnes Archer, OBE, MA(Oxon), D.Litt